12/20

D0071692

In memory of

Martin F. Buell, MD

And his wife,

Mary L. Buell

# THE WARRIOR CHALLENGE

## 8 QUESTS FOR BOYS TO GROW UP WITH KINDNESS, COURAGE, AND GRIT

**JOHN BEEDE**

ILLUSTRATED BY
JOHNNY DOMBROWSKI

RANDOM HOUSE 🏠 NEW YORK

All rights reserved. Published in the United States by Random House Children's Books,
a division of Penguin Random House LLC, New York.

Random House and the colophon are registered trademarks
of Penguin Random House LLC.

Visit us on the Web! rhcbooks.com

Educators and librarians, for a variety of teaching tools,
visit us at RHTeachersLibrarians.com

Library of Congress Cataloging-in-Publication Data is available upon request.
ISBN 978-0-593-17529-3 (trade) — ISBN 978-0-593-17530-9 (lib. bdg.) —
ISBN 978-0-593-17531-6 (ebook)

Printed in the United States of America
10 9 8 7 6 5 4 3 2 1
First Edition

FOR MY NEPHEW

—J.B.

# CONTENTS

**TRAINING PHASE I:** Weapons Mastery .......................................... 1

Challenge 1: Decide to Step Up ................................................... 3

Challenge 2: Become Self-Aware ................................................ 29

Challenge 3: Shift Your Finish Line ............................................. 57

**TRAINING PHASE II:** Defensive Upgrades .................................. 91

Challenge 4: Reinforce Your Armor ........................................... 93

Challenge 5: Form Your Battle Crew .......................................... 117

Challenge 6: Get Gritty .............................................................. 139

**TRAINING PHASE III:** Battle Tactics ...................................... 187

Challenge 7: Carry Antivenom ................................................ 189

Challenge 8: Choose Your Battleground .................................. 207

Resources ................................................................................ 237

Sources ................................................................................... 247

Acknowledgments ................................................................... 257

# TRAINING PHASE I

## WEAPONS MASTERY

When I was a kid, no one would tell me anything. I'd have questions about girls, about money, about life, about all this stuff. They'd tell me, "You're gonna find out."

I was like, "Man, if one person could just freakin' tell me what's going on, it would be really helpful." So I vowed that when I got to a position where people want to know and they ask me, I just tell 'em.

**—TERRY CREWS,**
**ACTOR, TV HOST, FORMER NFL PLAYER**

# CHALLENGE 1:
# DECIDE TO STEP UP

The highways of life are filled with flat
squirrels that couldn't make decisions.

**—JOHN MAXWELL,**
**AUTHOR AND LEADERSHIP SPEAKER**

# YOUR QUEST BEGINS

"Are you listening to me, boy?"

The man yelling at you is inches from your face. His eyes are wide and wild, and you can feel the heat of his breath on your cheek. You've never seen or met him before in your life. You have no idea who he is. His intensity makes you cringe and turn your head, taking in the inky darkness and feeling the soft dirt under your feet. It's just the two of you out here in the middle of nowhere, seemingly in the dead of night.

*Where the heck am I?*

Beside you, a blazing fire pops and sparks. You tense and find that you're sitting on . . . a hard stump of wood. *Am I . . . camping?* Your mouth is dry like sandpaper and your nostrils burn with dust and smoke.

"If you do not listen, you do not stand a chance," the man goes on. He imitates a knife slicing across his neck as he backs away from you, the motion drawing your attention to his bare, dark-skinned, muscular chest. The band around his head has . . . *Are those teeth?!* They're pointed upward like tiny menacing horns.

You try to find something familiar in your surroundings, but your eyes haven't fully adjusted to the darkness. Orange light flickers from the fire and illuminates a few nearby huts. Each is thatched together with branches and grass.

This sure isn't like the camping trips you went on when you were little. This feels very different. Like it's not about having fun.

"You'll be sent out soon," the man says as he circles you, thudding the handle of a spear with each step as he sizes you up.

"Which is why the village elders have tasked me with starting to train you."

*Train me? For what?* you wonder, the blood beginning to beat in your ears. *And . . . what in the . . . This dude has a legit spear?!*

"Take your weapon." He gestures to a second spear, its handle pushed into the earth next to you. The sharpened blade points to the stars of the galaxy above. They seem to be glowing more brightly than you've ever seen before.

"I crafted yours with wood of the ebony tree, bone of the wildebeest, and iron from the earth. It can kill an animal three times your size. Only true warriors are fit to carry this weapon. Make it your prized possession. But use it poorly, and you may injure yourself. Or worse . . ."

You look at the blade. It's as long as your leg.

You finally find your voice. "Who . . . who are you?" you ask.

"Me?" He laughs, full of pity. "I am your only hope. I am the only chance you have. I am the one who will guide you through this savanna, and I am the one who will teach you how to return alive from your quest."

"My quest?" you ask, feeling more deeply ensnared by each of his questions.

"Yes. Your quest to face the King of Beasts," the man says.

"Er, like a lion?"

"Is there any other King of Beasts?" he snaps. Then, lowering his voice: "I am Kakuta. I was chosen to be your Warrior Guide. Take your spear. Come now, take it! We don't have time for games."

You reach and slowly pull it from the earth. You feel its weight in your palm, which convinces you that you aren't dreaming. *This is mine?*

"Every warrior before you has completed a quest like the one in front of you. You must face and kill a lion. Learn, and you will survive, grow, and become strong. Succeed, and you will prove yourself worthy. You will be held in the highest respect. Our people will call you Warrior."

There is a pause. And the question falls out of your mouth: "And if I fail?"

"Then we will not call you anything," the man snarls, "because you will be dead. You will bring back the body of a lion, or—"

You dart your eyes anxiously, waiting.

After a beat, he finishes, "Or a lion will bring *your tattered body* back to its cubs. One way or another, one will die. And one will live."

You shake your head. *How can this be happening?!* You learned in biology that an adult male lion weighs, like, 420 pounds. They can leap up to thirty feet in the air and run faster than fifty miles per hour. What possible chance would you stand against an alpha predator like that? Even ten grown men would run for their lives if a lion was chasing them down the street!

Kakuta takes a step toward you. With each word, the tone of his voice becomes graver. "Do. You. Understand?"

You gulp and nod.

"Many have failed on this journey: Drowned by the raging floodwaters of the river. Mauled by the leopard. Some dropped dead with thirst. There are dangers all around. The one who is prepared to navigate all these challenges with honor—that is a man indeed."

The words ring in your head: "The one who is prepared to navigate all these challenges with honor—that is a man indeed."

You wonder, *Is that me?*

"You'll be sent out soon," he says, "so your training begins now.

I'll show you what I've learned about becoming a man in our village. But eventually, you must decide for yourself what defines you, for every boy must decide what kind of man he will become. Your first task is to learn to wield your spear. Try to use it on me! What kind of man will you be?"

To punctuate his speech, he adopts a defensive stance. "Your first task is to wield your spear. Go ahead!"

You stare at him blankly. You suddenly feel dizzy, overwhelmed. You look down at the ground and see the Adidas sneakers you bought last week. You're still wearing your jeans, your backpack, and the T-shirt your sister bought you for your birthday a few months ago. *What is going on?*

"You still with me? Hello?" The man twice thumps his spear in the dirt, which draws your eye to his sandals. Long brown hairs extend from the straps. They're made of animal hides. His toenails are the texture of cantaloupe skin, yellowed and corrugated.

Your gaze pans up his body; the fire's orange light casts dancing shadows over various scars on his limbs. Most obvious is his leg scar. It's thicker and deeper than any you've ever seen. It's as long as your forearm.

"That?" says Kakuta, pointing to the thick, tightened flesh of his old wound. "That is from my own training. I did not use my shield properly, and the spear of my sparring partner pierced my leg. It's a mistake I've never made twice." He lifts his spear, retracts it behind his body, and points the sharpened tip straight at your face. "Attack me with your spear!" His voice snaps like a whip. You hesitate to lift your spear in return.

He raises his voice as you falter. "Attack! Now!" He screams each syllable, the whites of his teeth flashing through the darkness. "Your training begins! Become a man!"

To punctuate his command, he suddenly stands tall, spinning the spear in his hands like an airplane propeller. The heavy iron blade smashes like a meteorite into the center of the fire, creating an explosion of burning embers. Missiles of hot coals fly at your body. You frantically brush at your lap and chest. You drop your spear in the same moment you smell your own burned hair. This does not feel like it's going well.

"Never drop your weapon. Your weapon is your life. Without it, you will be vulnerable to an increasingly dangerous world!" he yells.

Your nails scrape through the dirt as you grab your spear off of the ground. Your head swims. You feel hot with anger, and fear constricts your breath. *This isn't fair. I shouldn't be here! This isn't my life. I don't even know why I am supposed to fight this guy!*

He lifts his spear, again pointing it at you, seemingly about to—

"Help!" you yell, hoping that someone nearby will try to talk some sense into this guy. *"HELP!"*

Your only answer is the crackling of the fire. It's just you, Kakuta, and your spears. "Fight!" he yells.

He coils backward, his attack stance now familiar. *There's no choice but to fight back.* With the entirety of your might, you thrust your spear directly at his belly.

With impossible speed, he cracks his spear on top of yours. The

force of his parry is cataclysmic. You stumble forward, landing on your knees and elbows. A cloud of dust erupts around you. You've dropped your spear again.

"Good," he says, standing over you as you cough into the dirt. "You've begun your training. Yet you have much to learn about your mind. About your emotions. About your true strength. Much to learn about being a man."

Your embarrassment is overwhelming. *I could never be that strong. I'll never be that fast. I want to go home.* You crave your phone. Your video games. Your parents. Your bed. You'd take your boring math teacher over this guy any day of the week. *Anywhere is better than here.*

The fear is too much. You roll across the dirt, rise, and start to run. Running from the fire, from the warrior. With each frantic footfall, you reject his challenge to become a man. *What does that even mean?*

"Stop!" the warrior yells. "Return at once!" You ignore his calls as you hurtle yourself over a waist-high wooden fence. Your mind burns in unison with your heaving lungs.

You look over your shoulder and see that the warrior has not followed you over the fence but is still yelling. "Come back at once! Do not leave! I cannot help you out in the wild!"

*As if you were helping me in the first place, dude.*

You triple confirm that he's not following, then slow to a walk. Finally stopping to catch your breath, you drop your hands to your knees. *Okay, time to get home.*

Your focus is interrupted by a cackle of laughter. It comes from a hidden place in the darkness. But it's near.

You hold your breath and crouch to hide, as though the shrubbery can protect you. Your lungs feel like they might burst. The warrior begins screaming with a panicked intensity you've not yet heard from him. "Fight *me,* predator!" he pleads. "Take *me* instead!"

*Take me instead?*

The laughter overtakes Kakuta's voice, and two eyes appear right in front of you, glowing green. They're followed by sharp and exposed teeth. Then another set of eyes and teeth to the left. More to the right. Endless eyes and teeth emerge from the darkness, surrounding you.

You've left your spear in the village. You hear your guide's words echoing desperately in your mind: *"Your weapon is your life."*

You begin to make out the shapes of dozens of hyenas. They're pacing. Circling. Closing in, preparing to strike. Their symphony of snarls, growls, and laughter is the last thing you hear as they descend from all sides—

# KAKUTA HAMISI: AWAKEN YOUR WARRIOR

Look, kid. You have no idea how badly I wish that could be you and me in that scenario.

HEY. YOU. Are you listening? It's me, the author of the book you're reading. Snap out of it. My name is John. Better news? Chances are very high that no hyena is set to maul your face and no Maasai warrior is currently challenging you to a spear fight.

But you have no idea how badly, how urgently, I wish *I* could hold a spear to your face and—out of genuine, deep care and concern—train you to confront the metaphorical lions and hyenas in your life. Unfortunately, stabbing you with a spear is a crime in all fifty of the United States and every country, so this book is what we've got to work with.

Since we can't fly to Africa to spar together, we're gonna need a different place for our training grounds. That's what these pages are for. In them, you're going to discover how to navigate a wilderness that's different from the savanna but more real and more relevant to you. You'll learn how to attack, deflect, dodge, and eliminate the threats that exist in your hometown, even if you aren't sure what they are yet.

Real-life True Warrior Kakuta Ole Maimai Hamisi is the founder of the Maasai Association. Based in Kenya and Tanzania, his organization's purpose is to preserve the traditions of the Maasai people. His Maasai Warrior Training Experience simulates the education you would have received had you grown up in sub-Saharan Africa before 2008 (the year lion hunts were officially terminated). Until then, had you grown up in his culture, you'd have been required to complete a life-threatening lion hunt in order to be called a "man."

If you attend Kakuta's camp today, he'll make sure you won't be gobbled up by hyenas. He won't burn you with embers or injure you in any way. He'll train you to become an elite warrior, showing you how to throw a spear, defend yourself with a shield, track animals by their poop, build fires using friction, herd cattle, and survive in the African wilderness. In that part of the world, those are the skills required for manhood.

But what about where *you* live—what are the skills required to achieve manhood? If you don't feel there's a clear path in front of you for stepping up as a boy and growing into a man you're proud to be, you're not alone. It's a problem, for all of us.

Maybe you can relate to how I struggled when I was your age and tried figuring it out for myself. I was confused about dating.

About values. About sex. And, especially, about what it would take to make my life actually count for something. I had plenty of people around me who were excited to tell me all about math and English and marketable skills, but inside, I was like, "WILL SOME-BODY PLEASE JUST EXPLAIN WHAT THIS BECOMING-A-MAN STUFF IS ALL ABOUT?!"

Years later, after I'd fumbled my way to some of the answers, it occurred to me to ask the men and women in my life, "Hey, what do you think it means to be a quality man?" Whenever I met some-one with even halfway cool qualities, it became my go-to question, as second nature as "Hey, where ya from?" You could say I kinda went overboard, because by now, I've asked that question on every continent on Earth, including Antarctica.

While visiting his warrior camp in Kenya, I asked Kakuta what it means to be a man among the Maasai. He told me, "It means to step up and to step forward. A warrior decides to protect the soci-ety. And to not only defend a society in need, but to take care of the tasks of daily life."

He told me that the lion-hunting ritual was designed to teach a boy how to do those very things. The Maasai formula for manhood was simple but not easy: hunt a lion, become a man.

Weird as it might sound, after I heard that, I thought, *Why don't we have something like that? An awesome adventure every person goes on where somebody explains, super clearly, "Here's how to be self-sufficient. Here's how to defend your tribe. Here's how to decide what you want your life to be about."*

That question is why I set out to create a challenge that teaches those very things for dudes like you and me. I'll tell you up front . . . no joke . . . it became the most intense journey I've ever under-taken. If you're disappointed that a great African spear-fighting adventure isn't in store . . . don't be. In front of you is a wilderness with a greater set of challenges than Tanzania's Serengeti and Kenya's Maasai Mara combined.

You also have your own tribe. They are the people you interact with on a daily basis. They could be your classmates, your family, your teachers, your online community, your teammates, coaches, bus drivers, and store clerks. They don't have to be your closest friends; your tribe consists of the humans in your life. Beyond that, you are a part of a larger tribe of boys and men in general. To become a stand-up man among the warrior class, it's your job and mission to act as a leader and role model, protecting those in need. Your tribe needs you to be their champion.

*Protection from what?* you may ask. Trust me when I tell you that wild beasts and ruthless enemies still exist in your world. The ones you'll face won't have claws and fangs—which is precisely what makes them even more dangerous than Mufasa suntanning on Pride Rock. And because our enemies are different, we need a different set of weapons. Kakuta's advice about stepping up still holds true for you: *Learn and you will survive, grow, and become strong.*

In fact, that is your first challenge for becoming a True Warrior:

**Challenge 1: Make the choice to step up. Make the decision to start training to hunt *your* King of Beasts. That's where you have to begin if you want a chance at handling yourself in the wild and defending your tribe. You'll know you've succeeded at this challenge when you've made the choice to initiate your training.**

If that feels like a lot, you can take a deep breath. This book is *not* going to be full of cheesy and outdated stereotypes about manhood—I'm not going to give you advice like "grow a lumberjack beard" or "buy a great set of power tools." If you never grow up to smoke cigars and play poker in a basement man cave, that's fine by me. If you never drive a 4x4 lifted truck through an explosion while one of your buddies shoots clay pigeons with a shotgun and your other buddy grills steaks in the truck bed . . . well, I'll be sad that you missed out on that. But you're still good in my book.

In our culture, we have a lot of bizarre ideas about what's manly. When you succeed at this challenge, it means you'll start considering the question: *What kind of person would I be proud of becoming?* You are the hero of this story, after all. Each step along the path is yours. I'm simply your Warrior Guide.

Which perhaps has you wondering . . . *Mmmkay, dude, who are you to be my Warrior Guide?*

Bluntly, here's who I am: I've climbed the tallest mountains on all seven continents. Which includes summiting Mount Everest. I've kitesurfed ocean waves three times my height in the South China Sea. I've swum with sharks, jumped out of airplanes, and practiced yoga on remote islands. I've been to sixty-four countries and counting . . . and paid for my travels and adventures by starting, managing, and selling businesses. I've been struck by lightning. I've been trapped in the Indonesian jungle between warring tribes and the world's largest gold mine. It's been a wild ride.

By many people's standards, that's a pretty manly list of accomplishments.

But for me, nothing on that list defines me as a man. That's just the highlight reel—no mistakes, scars, or heart-wrenching stuff.

If I'm asking you to get real, then I gotta start by being fully, completely real with you. Here's what's un-Superman-like about me: I've screwed up. A lot. I've unintentionally hurt people. I've been homeless. I had malaria attacks for over a year. I was in a rollover car accident. I've been heartbroken, depressed, and panicked. I've been assaulted. I've grieved. I've felt scared and lonely. Some days it's been *really* hard to get out of bed.

Nobody's perfect, myself definitely included. But by taking baby steps each day of my life, I slowly plowed through that tough stuff. That's what makes me more of a man right now, today, than when I stood on top of Mount Everest.

So unlike that garbage superhero named Superman who has no flaws and is only weak to a space rock that doesn't even exist, I want you to know that I bleed. I make mistakes.

And it's okay if you do, too.

I'm not asking you to be perfect because there *is* no such thing as perfect. Instead, I am asking you to make the choice to step up and improve. Decide to up your game by becoming a high-quality person. It's not about accomplishing mind-boggling feats—it's about living by your values.

This book isn't another list of impossible standards that will just make you feel guilty. It's also not ever going to make you feel ashamed just for being a guy. Nope. None of that.

Instead, this is about committing to becoming a little bit better, even if it's just a little bit at a time. But that doesn't mean it'll be easy. Far from it. It'll be raw. This is about getting real. Think you're up for that?

Along with the quests that make up *The Warrior Challenge*, you can consider this book to be the man-to-man fireside chat that your parents and teachers can't have with you, but perhaps secretly wish they could.

Here's the deal: if there's a parent or adult you respect and trust, I highly recommend that you ask them to read this book with you. Man or woman, their experience and knowledge will help you become an even more powerful Warrior. That adult can also be your Warrior Guide. So think of who it could be, then show them this paragraph and ask if they'll be that person for you.

Either way, your journey begins like all Warrior journeys: when you step up in your heart and say, "I've decided to start improving. I'll probably make mistakes, but I'll use what I learn to keep growing into a better man." Once you make that decision, you're in. Welcome to the team, Warrior. You're officially a Warrior Apprentice! Woot woot!

Here's what your training consists of: Remember how I went around asking everybody, "What makes a man?" Well, I took everybody's answers . . . PLUS the info from the piles of books I devoured . . . PLUS my own wild life experiences . . . and I noticed something kinda weird. There was a pattern. The same eight character traits kept popping up!

But who wants a dumb list of eight things to memorize?

A story is way better than a list. And what's even better than a story is eight jaw-dropping, ridiculously gnarly stories from people who inspire me beyond belief. People who are pretty much regular dudes, just like you and me, but who act like superheroes.

Your challenge is to be like these eight dudes I talk about in the rest of the book. Aspire to their greatness. Most never fought in battles or wielded weapons, yet I consider these men to be some of the greatest warriors who have ever lived. Your challenge is to stand for what they stand for and embody what they embody. Do that, and you will become a warrior as well.

# LEVEL UP YOUR WARRIOR

Your quest? Embrace the epic traits of all eight of our True Warriors. Own them. Make them yours. Figure out what they mean when it comes to your school, your family, the people you hang out with, the people you date, the goals and dreams you chase. Embrace all eight qualities on your terms and you'll become a True Warrior. You'll have everything you need to consider yourself a man in the best way, in your home, village, town, city, country, and— seriously—anywhere on the planet. That's how you can level up your warrior.

Same as in video games, the challenges that make up this rite of passage are laid out in increasing levels of difficulty. Each of the eight True Warriors whose lives you'll experience exemplifies one of the eight traits. And just as it is with first-person video games, you're going to see the action *through their eyes. You're gonna DO their epic thing,* just like you did with Kakuta. You're going to *experience* what it's like to think, feel, and act like . . . and BE a True Warrior. You think you're up for the challenge?

# WORLD TOUR

Do you know what your life would be like, right now, at your age, if you grew up in another time and another place? If you had to prove to your family, and to your whole society, that you have what it takes to be a man, do you know what you'd have to do? Let me take you around the world to show you.

We'll start in New Zealand. In the ancient Maori tribes, a boy had to get ink burned into his face with hot, sharp needles. That means that to become a man, you would've needed to get an unsterilized face tattoo.

Ouch.

Now let's fly into the desert of the Australian outback. Had you grown up here as an Aboriginal, they would have sent you into the desert for up to six months to survive on your own. If you didn't come back . . . shucks. Seems you weren't a man after all!

And aren't you glad that, to call yourself a man in the twenty-first-century, you don't have to engage in a whipping battle like the Fula people of Sudan and Senegal? Or run naked across the backs of furious, freshly castrated bulls like the Hamar tribe in Ethiopia?

Our next stopover is Vanuatu, a chain of South Pacific islands. Were this your home, to be considered a man you'd be required to climb a hundred-foot-tall tree in a practice called land diving. After you reach the treetop, the village elders would tie vines to your legs. After the vines were good and snug, you'd need to leap headfirst toward the ground. You wouldn't dare hesitate. After all, the point of this rite is to prove that you don't fear death. You'd leap and se-cretly hope the vines would catch your body weight—but not too soon, because the closer your head comes to the ground, the more of a man you're considered.

Finally, let's go east and cross the Pacific Ocean, stopping in the depths of Brazil's Amazonian rainforest. To this day, the Mawé tribe forces its boys to experience the worst pain the jungle has to offer. Aspiring men have to endure the sting of the bullet ant, proven to be the most painful bite of any insect on Earth. Chemist Dr. Anne Marie Helmenstine describes the pain as being "blinding, electric, and comparable to being shot with a gun."

In fact, according to the Schmidt Sting Pain Index, the bullet ant bite is twenty times more painful than the hornet's sting—and out of 91,000 species of insects in our world, only three have bites that are even in the same category of pain. In fact, the bullet ant sting doesn't hurt for just a few minutes. Not even just a couple of hours. Nope. The bullet ant sting lasts for . . . Twenty. Four. Hours.

In that time, waves of excruciating pain come and go. Each one rocks the nervous system violently enough to knock a human out cold. The bites are so painful that some men will hallucinate as a coping mechanism because their brains can't process that level of pain. The bites can even paralyze a jaguar!

But the Mawé boys aren't stung just once. Oh, no. That's too easy. The elders stitch together a glove made of leaves and weave bullet ants into the glove. The boys are then forced to wear the glove for five full minutes as ants sting them again and again.

I can guarantee you this: In the first of the twenty-four hours of the vomit-inducing pain inflicted by these ants, there's at least one moment in that kid's mind when he's saying to himself, *I can't handle this any longer! It has to stop! It hurts too much!*

And yet, when the pain subsides, the boy sees that he could, in fact, handle it. Turns out he was wrong about what he was capable of.

But it doesn't stop there. The boys then go through this ordeal and wear the ant-filled glove twenty separate times over the course of several months.

Yeah. You read that right. Twenty. Separate. Ordeals.

By that twentieth time, that kid's surely got a different voice in his head. It's more like *I was wrong about myself before. Now I know for a fact I've got this. In fact, if these puny ants are the worst thing in the jungle, that sucks for the jungle, because they're nothing compared to me. I can protect my people from any other threat that might arise.*

*That's* a man. He believes that the greatest threats in his wilderness ain't got jack on him . . . because he's proven it.

Here's my question for you: Can you say that about yourself? Are you confident that you can defend yourself and your tribe from the worst that your world has to offer?

# WARRIOR BOOT CAMP

Fortunately for humanity, about a hundred years ago people started thinking, *Hey, maybe these life-threatening trials aren't the best way to help our kids grow up.* And these rites were stopped altogether.

That's a huge win for you! You hit the human history jackpot!

But why establish these rites of passage in the first place?

We can actually get the answer by just looking at the term itself:

The fancy-pants Latin root for the word "rite" is *ritualis.* That's also where we get the word "ritual" from. Feel free to impress your English teacher with that one. You're welcome.

And "passage" means to go from one place to another. A "rite of passage," then, is a ritual in which a boy makes the transition from boyhood to manhood.

If we take away the tree jumping and skin mutilation and naked bull running, what's left over? What did ALL the rites of passage have in common? What did they have right that we should still strive for, today?

I totally nerded out looking for the answer. I graphed every rite of passage that I could find throughout human history and found what I was looking for: three universal themes in every single rite of passage . . . ever. In fact, I can't find a single culture in history that doesn't consider each of these human qualities to be friggin' awesome:

1. Mastery of your mind—or yourself.
2. Mastery of your heart—or how you relate to others.
3. Mastery of your guts—or your actions in the world.

BOOM. That's what it takes.

# WHAT DOES A TRUE WARRIOR LOOK LIKE?

I have mentioned women and girls exactly zero times so far. If you noticed that and wondered why, I suspect that you're already on to an unfortunate truth: Human history has been sexist.

Mmmmkay . . . *So why is this book geared toward guys? Isn't that also sexist?*

Half of why this is a book for guys is because I'm a guy. I'm a straight white dude. Even though I read about, listen to, and am curious about all people I meet, I haven't lived everybody's experience and can't pretend to have. I can't change who I am, and I don't want to be someone I'm not. Because of that, I can't pretend to understand what it's like to be a woman in today's world. When it comes to this stuff, the only thing I can say for sure is that I get what it's like to be a guy in our world. So I'm starting with dudes because that's where I have my own experience.

The other half? This book is geared toward guys because women deserve better men. In my opinion it's women who are stepping up and taking on the role of True Warriors at a clip that we guys aren't keeping up with. That doesn't mean we gotta surpass them to win. No, man, that's literally the opposite of what I'm saying. I'm saying that guys and girls alike need to progress at equal speeds.

While it's true that these three ancient warrior themes of masculinity were originally intended for the men of a tribe, this isn't an all-boys club any longer. So if you're reading this and you're one gender or no gender or every gender, know that it truly, from the bottom of my soul, does not make a difference to me.

Bottom line: These quests are for any human being who wants to make the most of their life. These quests are about how to become a person of character. Nobody is excluded just because of their body parts.

# EXPECT SCARS

When you imagine a True Warrior, please don't imagine some knight in shining armor riding a white horse. That warrior isn't real. He's boring, lame, a snore. No thanks, bro.

Instead, imagine Kakuta. He has that giant scar on his leg from when he made a mistake with his shield. He may have messed up, but it's a mistake he never made twice. That's how the *heart* of a True Warrior learns—by owning mistakes and committing to doing better next time. True Warriors are gritty. Think: covered in mud and scars, and savvier because they've learned that the world is a complicated, unpredictable place. Nobody is perfect at these challenges the first time around. Probably never perfect.

That includes me. I haven't always known these things. I've made mistakes. I've even accidentally hurt other people while figuring this stuff out. One billion percent, I'm not here standing on a pedestal wearing a cape, clenching my fist in the air, shouting, "Aspire to be like me! I've perfected these challenges!"

Far from it.

Succeeding at this challenge is more about being willing to start trying. You don't have to be perfect. But you've gotta agree that, as men, we can be better. That starts with you making the choice for yourself to step up and start being a part of the solutions in the world, not a part of the problems.

Really get that—and do that—and you'll succeed at Challenge 1.

Choose to not get that or do that and it'll be like playing *Mario Kart* in 200cc mode without first building up your skill level to match that speed. You're gonna crash and burn in a really big way. Life will get ahead of you. And you know how that goes: Play a level before you're ready, and the game becomes frustrating and not very fun.

All the pressure you feel—the pressure to fit in, succeed, man up, make something of yourself—all that needs to go somewhere. But without a clearly defined path for becoming a man, we've got what former President Barack Obama described as "a recipe for disaster." He explained: "In every society, young men are going to have violent tendencies. Either those tendencies are directed and disciplined in creative pursuits or those tendencies destroy the young men, or the society, or both."

Bingo, Barack.

That *has* been a disaster.

Until now.

# YOUR TRAINING BEGINS

You're growing up. Right now. As you read this, love it or hate it, it's happening. This book is your clearly defined path for becoming a man.

You think you're up for the challenge?

Let's go back to Kakuta to find out. Right now, your weapon is on the ground. You're on your hands and knees, coughing up a cloud of dust in the firepit. You consider running.

But then you see your spear. It's your choice to grip the handle. That weapon can be yours if you take it. *Will you?*

You look up and see Kakuta, the Maasai warrior. The orange firelight flickers, glinting on the blade of his spear. His hand is extended, offering to help you stand.

Will you decide to step up? Will you step forward and begin the Warrior Challenge?

If your answer is "Yes," you have officially passed Challenge 1.

Play the victory music as Mario slides down the flagpole! Drop the checkered flags, shoot off the fireworks, and cue the slow golf claps!

You've just begun one heck of an adventure. There are seven more challenges before you reach the finish line, and each challenge will be more difficult than the one before.

Don't worry, I've got your back as you train to become a True Warrior. You're gonna become a real beast of a man *and* a good human being, all at once.

Your weapon is your life. Your training begins.

# TRAINING GROUNDS:
## DECIDE TO STEP UP

At the end of each challenge, you'll find a Training Grounds section like this one. Each will start with a bottom-line summary of the concept of the challenge, to ensure that you KNOW IT. Like this:

## *KNOW IT*

A boy lets other people determine who he'll grow up to become. A man decides to do whatever it takes to become his best self and defend his tribe.

After you Know It, it's time to Act On It, proving to yourself and the world that you've passed the challenge. That's why, for each section, I've given you a checklist of three steps you can take in order get started immediately. If you want to compete in expert mode, put your initials in the boxes after you complete the tasks!

# ACT ON IT

☐ Commit, right now, to finishing all eight challenges in this book. Say yes to the rite of passage that's in front of you. You've already passed Challenge 1—commit to "step up" to the seven that remain!

☐ Think of an adult in your life you admire. Text them, message them, or tell them in person that you'd like to become a True Warrior. Ask them if they'd be willing to help you along the way. Ask if they'll read this book with you and guide you through each of the challenges.

☐ Give yourself a word of encouragement. Say to yourself, in your own words, *Way to go*. And while you're at it, be proud of yourself. You are on the right track.

P.S. For anyone interested, in the back of the book you'll find my research, source material, and supporting books, expert citations, and articles.

## THAT'S IT! PROCEED TO CHALLENGE 2!

# CHALLENGE 2: BECOME SELF-AWARE

Because he believes in himself,
He doesn't try to convince others.
Because he is content with himself,
He doesn't need others' approval.
Because he accepts himself,
The whole world accepts him.

*—LAO TZU,*
*THE TAO TE CHING*

# MAN OF COURAGE

Hobbling on your fractured ankle, you make your way through a maze of metal scaffolding. It smells like freshly cut wood and welded piping. You are underneath the largest skate park ever built: the Beijing MegaRamp. It's a 121-foot-tall roll-in leading to a kicker that will launch you over the gutsiest gap ever conceived. This enormous, beautiful ramp was built only for you.

You reach the staircase that leads to the top and place your foot on the first step. Shooting nerve pain lights up your body and reverberates in your spine with each step. *Yep, still broken.* Swollen and throbbing, the fractured ankle belongs to your very important steering leg.

You breathe, switching the focus away from your pain, trying to get in the zone. You've heard that scientists call it being in "flow." Whatever it's called, you'd better get there. Quickly. This is the biggest day of your life, and perhaps the biggest single day in the history of skateboarding.

Back in the United States, authorities would never have allowed something like this ramp to be constructed. No American crew would ever have agreed to build it because to anyone except the world's most elite extreme athletes, it looks like a fatality waiting to happen.

But here in China, sixty workers labored for weeks in 106-degree heat to build the most epic jump sequence of all time. It's made of two truckloads of scaffolding, enough plywood to cover several tennis courts, and so many screws that, when they ran out, there were none of the right size left in all of China. They had to complete the top of the structure using nails instead, which could pop out at any second. *Super sketchy!* you think, feeling the drop-in tower wobble as you ascend each flight of stairs.

In the end, though, the sheer size of this record-setting skate ramp isn't what matters. What matters is what you're going to do with it. It was built for the sole purpose of giving you speed. A lot of it. When you hit the lip of the first booster, you'll hurtle into the air and hopefully clear the enormous gap. Then, if you manage to stick the landing, you'll hold the record for the longest jump on a skateboard. Ever.

It's hot and the air is thick. Light through the clouds makes you squint as you catch glimpses of your obstacle, visible between the metal bars. Dragonflies buzz near your face and drown out the shouts of the crowds in the stands. Behind them is the legendary, enormous stone structure curving its way up the tree-covered mountainside— perhaps the most famous wall in the world. It's actually a network of ancient trade and war barriers that totals 13,170 miles long, longer than the distance from the North Pole to the South Pole. One thing is for certain: the ancient soldiers who originally built it never could have imagined what you're going to attempt in a few moments.

You're about to jump over the Great Wall of China. On a skateboard!

Your original plan was to clear the widest part of the wall—a sixty-foot horizontal distance. *Wouldn't have done my sport justice to jump a skinny section.* But a mistake in the ramp's construction was discovered just days ago. Your team called you with panicked voices, telling you the foundations were set too far apart. Then they basically asked: "Is it okay that we accidentally added an extra fifteen feet of distance, making it world-record setting?" Meaning now you needed to clear a seventy-five-foot-wide gap . . . or else become a pancake.

Something in your nineteen years of professional experience as a skateboarder told you that it was still doable. Phone to your ear, you said back: "Nothing's too gnarly. I've got this," and hung up.

Yesterday, you decided to take a practice run. Just like the ones you'd taken back home as you trained for this. But what you never considered was that those practice jumps were in the desert, where the air was dry. Here in central China, the air's thick humidity creates resistance. That resistance slowed you down so much yesterday that you smashed into the deck three feet short of your landing ramp. Your foot crumpled underneath your body's impact, flipping you head over feet, tossing you down the ramp like a flicked penny. "Rag-dolling," as it's called in your world. Eventually, you came to a lifeless stop in the ramp's trough.

"I can't steer the board if I'm wearing a cast," you told your team as they rushed you to the hospital. That's why you refused an X-ray; you didn't want a diagnosis resulting in a treatment that would make steering the board—and the jump—impossible.

Despite the injury, there was no way to postpone. All the permits were in place. The ramp was built. Media reporters had flown in from around the world. Chinese citizens were instructed to take off work. It was now or never.

But you needed more speed. Overnight, engineers scrambled to build an extension for the drop-in. A taller structure would equal more speed, and more speed would equal a longer jump. They figured the extra ten feet of height would help create the momentum needed to clear the extra three feet of distance.

That's why you're now climbing up an even taller tower. If you manage to stick the landing, on the other side of the wall there's a thirty-two-foot-tall quarter pipe. It's there to slow you down. You'll be bombing at fifty miles an hour, so if you hit the lip clean, the math says you'll launch seventy feet into the air. That'll be your opportunity to set your *second* world record for the *highest* jump on a skateboard. *I'm gonna jump to the height of a seven-story building!*

These are your own records you're attempting to beat, which makes sense—for you, it's never been about competing against anyone else. It's always been about discovering what's possible for yourself. It's about digging deep and seeing what you're made of.

As you climb each flight of stairs, you get deeper into the zone. You scan your body from head to toe, building a mental picture of yourself and your surroundings. The tower wobbles a little more, like it's trying to shake you off. Like it's telling you, "No. You can't do this. You're not enough. You'll never be good enough."

Closing your eyes, you focus on taking a long, deep, controlled breath. You realize it's not the humongous skate ramp that's saying those things. No, the monster talking smack is the voice inside your head. You tell it it's wrong: *I am more than my negative voices. I am not my thoughts.*

As your eyelids flutter open, you see a mob of spectators in the packed stands. It's a mix of people who would never otherwise come together—hundreds of Chinese government officials and dozens of the skateboarding buddies you've met along your journey as a pro. They're finally able to spot you climbing the ramp, and their cheering grows louder.

That's when something completely unexpected happens.

*Thousands* of people start emerging from the bushes in unison! They'd apparently been hiding from security all along, and they're now making it look as if the ground itself is moving.

And they're not the only ones watching. There are 125 million people currently tuned in all across the world, watching you climb these steps. DC Shoes, one of your sponsors, created the position of the "Chinese Minister of Extreme Sports." And the "minister" even filmed a broadcast of himself speaking to the whole country. He told them to rearrange their work schedules because of you: "Man of Courage will jump our Great Wall of China!"

*No pressure, dude.*

Now all those people are going to see either an amazing feat . . . or total carnage. Because there's no denying it: this could end your life. The last person who tried to jump the Wall without a motor was mountain biker Wang Jiaxiong three years ago, and he tragically overshot the landing, lost control in the air, and fell fifty feet. Later that day he died of internal injuries. Nobody has tried since.

Suddenly, there aren't any more stairs for you to climb. Scaling ten flights in the hot and humid air has exhausted you. You shove your helmet on top of your sweaty mop of brown hair as the dragonflies buzz even faster around your head.

*What if one hits me in the eye on the way down? Or flies into my mouth?*

You push your one good leg firmly into the surface of the platform. The whole tower sways in reaction. Your body lurches side to side along with it. *Uh, this thing is definitely* not *built properly!* You snap your helmet buckle as you look down. There it is: a ten-story drop-in leading straight toward the Great Wall of China.

The crowd comes to a hush. Your whole life has led up to this moment. This is when you get to show your people, your tribe, the worldwide skateboarding community what's possible. *This is new territory*, you realize. *This is the land of the unknown. I'm experimenting with things that seem impossible and I'm defining what's possible. This is my chance to prove what I've believed all along: Nothing's too gnarly.*

Closing your mind to your surroundings, you drown out all distractions. *The only thing I'm going to do right now is put my board down, stand on it, and jump that thing.*

You push off.

Leaning forward, you hear a sound you love—polyurethane wheels rolling over plywood. It intensifies, getting louder and more high-pitched as you break the Guinness record for speed on a skateboard. It's music to your ears. You hit the lip of the ramp. In the same moment that your back wheels clear the coping, everything becomes silent.

Time is standing still. You're suspended in the sky. Your awareness expands beyond yourself to the enormous temple next to you, guarded by ancient stone statues. You see each of the thousands of illegal spectators, every camera and every hopeful skater watching through their screens from around the world. You think of your father, whose ashes you have in your pocket. You wanted to take him with you, show him what it's like up here, in the zone.

Then, from forty feet in the air, you spot the landing.

*Nothing's too gnarly. I've got this.*

# DANNY WAY: SEE YOURSELF

True Warrior Danny Way stuck the landing. On a fractured foot.

You'd think that would have been enough. You know, setting the world-record distance jump on a skateboard—over the Great Wall of China.

But for him, it wasn't enough. Because Danny didn't stick the *second* landing. That quarter pipe as tall as three and a half basketball hoops. The same one that rocket-shipped him up to the world's *tallest* skateboarding jump. Danny lost control in midair and fell, sliding safely down the ramp.

That's when 125 million people got to see how to pass our second challenge here. Danny became self-aware. He knew he was capable of more.

See, that first jump was successful by anyone's standards. Danny's sponsors were happy. The crowds were thrilled. His name was locked down as legendary in the history of skateboarding. Nobody needed anything more from him. Everyone knew his ankle was broken, after all. But meeting other people's standards wasn't what he came for. He was there to prove to *himself,* and to hopeful skaters around the world, what's possible.

Danny Way is one of the most revered names in skateboarding, not only because he's won every major skateboarding competition in existence or because he once leapt out of a helicopter with only his skateboard and no parachute. Those were cool feats, but Danny inspires awe because for him, it's not about grunting through his pain or trying to prove himself to anyone but *himself*. He already held the world records he was breaking. And he had already made the jump!

He held himself to his own standard of excellence. Not anyone else's. Sure, his ankle was in excruciating pain. Sure, he was scared. But he knew he had what it would take to succeed. He knew he could stick the second landing despite pain, despite fear, and despite what anyone else had to say about his sanity. *He could see it.* For a professional with this level of skill, the obstacles were an afterthought.

So Danny stood up, grabbed his skateboard, and started walking back toward the roll-in. With a deep breath, he said to himself, *Nothing's too gnarly. I've got this.*

This is a trait that defines Danny Way as a man: He's able to "see himself" and what he's capable of. It's in the zone that he's able to shift his attention away from fear and self-doubt and focus on pushing the limits of what's possible. That's exactly what your next challenge is all about!

> **Challenge 2 is to become self-aware. You must develop the ability to see yourself in any given moment. That's how you can get in the zone, understand what you're made of, and influence the world. You will know that you've succeeded at this challenge the moment you begin to utilize self-intel-gathering techniques and separate your mind's helpful thoughts from the not-so-helpful.**

So there went Danny, hobbling back across the Great Wall of China and arriving at the base of the launch ramp. He again used his broken ankle to climb 121 feet of stairs leading to the top of the tower. Once there, he leaned forward and rolled down the ramp. Reaching critical, breakneck speed in seconds, he launched himself over the Great Wall for a second time. Only now, Danny blew the minds of everyone watching when he threw a perfect 360 over the gap!

With a crack like a gunshot, the wheels of his board clacked against the wood of the landing ramp. He stuck the landing! The crowd was cheering so loud that the whole skate structure rumbled. But Danny didn't even notice, because he was focused on one thing: the quarter pipe. He leaned into his speed, gaining even more of it on the downhill.

That's how the impossible happened. Danny hit the quarter pipe and catapulted into the air. At the apex of his jump, he grabbed his board and showboated for the crowd, extending the other arm to the sky. Seventy feet in the sky, gravity curbed his floating sensation and he began to plunge thirty-eight feet back toward the metal edge of the ramp. He effortlessly positioned the deck of his board underfoot and, despite four Gs (forces of gravity) on a broken ankle, he nailed the second landing! Absolutely unbelievable, especially when you realize that space shuttles only generate three Gs when launching and most humans black out when they experience five gravities.

*Surely, now he's done,* the crowd must have thought. After all, he just stuck both landings and set two world records in a single run!

But it's not every day that they build a half-million-dollar ramp for the greatest skateboarder alive. Plus he needed his tribe to know that what had just happened wasn't a fluke or a lucky landing. So Danny turned around and made the potentially lethal jump again. And again. And again. *Five total times* he climbed the wobbling tower and cleared the Great Wall of China on his fractured ankle. Because of this feat, Danny is one of three people who have their names engraved in gold on the Great Wall of China.

Danny will tell you that he's "human like everyone else" and that he "feels pain in the same way everyone else does." Which is his way of saying that you're just as capable of accessing the same level of self-awareness and getting yourself in the zone. Keep in mind that Danny had nineteen years of experience as a professional skateboarder before this stunt. That's more time spent skating than you've been alive! That means he was precisely tuned in to his body's messages and knew exactly what it was capable of. But you? Hear me when I say that you definitely do not need to break a bone, complete death-defying stunts, or withstand any level of physical pain in order to become a man.

Here's why Danny's story matters to you: Self-awareness is about learning to recognize and understand the messages your thoughts, body, and emotions are sending to you. Self-awareness is the first step to mastering any skill. Knowing when it's time for rest and healing is a massive part of that!

In this challenge, you're going to learn to get in the zone for whatever you want—sports, pop quizzes, conversation, music . . . anything in life. Once you're able to get there, you will be able to push your abilities—and your limits—with the things *you* love and with the things *you* are passionate about. You can show your tribe what's possible if you learn to think like Danny Way.

It all starts with becoming self-aware.

# YOUR SUPERHUMAN SUPERPOWER

In Challenge 1, you chose to step up. Yet there is a zero percent chance that any growth or change is gonna happen unless you can clearly see and be aware of what's going on inside yourself from moment to moment. That skill is the foundation for *every single challenge ahead of you.* You need to be able to accurately name the emotions you're feeling, separate yourself from all the thoughts swimming around in your head, and then observe what's physically going on in your body.

If you think of yourself as a Warrior stationed at a base camp, then being self-aware is the most important cornerstone of your Warrior Base Camp. Because without self-awareness, there is no growth, no pushing your limits, no becoming a better man.

I can hear you thinking. *Name my emotions? Watch my thoughts? Observe my body? A little woo-woo here, bro.*

I get it. "Seeing yourself" might sound a little out there. Just in case you've started wondering, *Has this climber dude spent too much time at high altitude and lost some important brain cells?* here's why this is a critical foundation for all warriors:

Without being self-aware, there is absolutely no way to be honest. Not with yourself. And not with anyone else. Meaning, if you fail to see yourself, you stand no chance of knowing your own truth. And without knowing your truth, how can you possibly speak it to others?

Without passing this challenge, you're oblivious. To yourself. And to others.

Becoming self-aware isn't an idea I randomly came up with. Seeing yourself is a skill that True Warrior guides like me have taught their apprentices as far back as written human history goes . . . and right up to *Star Wars*.

Plato and Socrates, two of the wisest dudes in ancient Greece, are both credited with teaching their students to "know thyself." Fast-forward to one of the greatest modern-day martial artists, Bruce Lee. He said, "You have the truth within. I can't teach you anything new, only remind you of what you already know to be true. To know your own truth, you need to learn to look within." Virginia Woolf, one of the most important and influential authors of the twentieth century, said, "Without self-awareness we are as babies in the cradles." In other words: if you fail to see yourself, you'll be trapped as a boy for life.

I rest my case.

So, how's this self-awareness business done? Let me take you down the rabbit hole of awesomeness. . . .

# WHO YOU REALLY ARE

Can you think of a time when you doubted whether you could accomplish something but then proved yourself wrong? A situation where you didn't think you could run another step, pass a test, or even get to school on time?

Your mind said that you couldn't do the thing.

But then you did the thing.

This proves that *you are not your thoughts*.

Everybody has dark clouds roll through their minds. Me included.

That voice in our heads can be really horrible. It can say nasty, brutal things. For most of us, we let that inner voice trash-talk us with things we'd never dream of saying to anyone else. Worse, we're so used to it happening that we usually don't even notice!

And if you're like every other human on the planet, it's not just your thoughts. It's your emotions that can be negative, too. We can experience hatred. We get frustrated. We doubt ourselves. We get angry. Feeling these things doesn't make you a bad person or somehow weird or broken. The opposite, actually. These are normal feelings, and they're all part of being human. But they don't define you. They are not *you*.

You are not your pain; that goes away. You are not your life history; that's in the past. You are not your emotions; those change. You are not your anxiety; that's your worries about the future.

Which probably leaves you thinking: *Okay, but if I'm not those things,* then who am I?

You are not the thoughts swarming around in your head. *You are the one who hears them.* You are not the emotions surging in your heart. *You are the one who feels them.* You are not even your physical sensations. *You are the one who experiences them.*

Your thoughts, your emotions, and your five physical senses? They're just like pesky little messengers, reporting back to you about what's going on in base camp. Sometimes they're helpful, sometimes they're annoying. Sometimes accurate. Sometimes totally full of it. But no matter what, they are eagerly doing their job. That is, they all report to YOU, the head honcho in the war seat. You are the one who's in charge of gathering intel from what your heart, mind, and body are saying. And then, using all the combined info, THAT'S when you decide what's *really* going on. To do that, you gotta listen to the information you're getting without instantly reacting to it!

# YOUR INNER ROOMMATE

The problem is that the negative voice in your head never shuts up! It seriously just blabs on and on. It talks so much that we fall into the trap of thinking that we are what it says to us. It has us fooled!

Michael A. Singer, in his book *The Untethered Soul,* calls this voice "your inner roommate." He says that your roommate has an opinion about everything and, often, your roommate talks just for the sake of talking.

I mean, have you ever listened to what's going on inside your own brain? *Hey, cool sneakers. I should get new sneakers. Eh, look at this guy. What's his deal? Did I remember my homework? I'm hungry. Man, I gotta pee. I can't wait for the bell to ring. I like bells. Ding! I can't believe what my sister's going through. I wonder what Kelly's up to. Dude, I gotta scratch my crotch but people are around. Whoa, that's a weird smell. Who made that? Okay, back to this geography test. . . .*

It's endless! Let me ask you: If you literally had somebody sitting next to you who talked like that all day, every day, wouldn't that drive you bonkers? I'd want to strangle that person! "Stop the insanity!" I'd yell.

So which of all these nonstop voices is actually *you*? According to Singer, "The answer is simple: none of them." Instead, you are the one who sees your thoughts.

*Mmmmkay, what does THAT mean?*

For example, Danny Way chose to replace his negative thoughts with more empowering beliefs: "Nothing's too gnarly. I've got this."

True Warriors do the same. They just observe what's going on inside their heads—they simply receive the intel. Then, when they see a negative thought or emotion, they replace it with a better option!

In other words, as a Warrior, you can hijack your own brain. Which is what I like to call: roommate sabotage.

Okay, so you've got this roommate inside who won't shut up. And a lot of the time, that jerk can be really negative. Unfortunately, that's just reality. . . . Which means it's up to you to decide what you're gonna do about it.

I once had an actual flesh-and-blood roommate who always wanted to one-up me. About. Everything.

If I said I stubbed my toe, he'd say that he broke his foot. If I said I'd just finished reading a book, he'd say he'd just finished writing a book.

Have you ever met someone like this?

So I picked up on his pattern and started playing a good-hearted trick on him. I'd only tell him positive things. Like this:

ME: "Hey, dude, I woke up in a great mood today."

HIM: "Yeah? Well, I woke up feeling freaking phenomenal. I'm actually going for a run."

ME: "I bet that'll be a lot of fun. I love running in the sunshine."

HIM: "You don't even know, dude. It's gonna be like sunshine is shooting out of my face. It's going to be the best run of my life."

And off he went on the best run of his life, solar radiation shooting out of his face.

See what I did? I sabotaged my flesh-and-blood roommate to

have better thoughts. And that's exactly what you can do with your inner roommate.

When you doubt whether you can accomplish something, all you have to do is observe. Simply watch that unrelenting voice. "See" the chatter inside your head. Remember, you're not judging what it says. You're not getting sucked into its negativity.

If you're having trouble with this, brilliant brain researcher Dr. Mithu Storoni, author of *Stress Proof,* suggests that you hold a very simple balancing position. It could be a plank or even standing on one leg. You'll soon notice that your brain starts screaming at you. "Stop! You aren't capable of this! You can't keep going!" you'll hear it say.

But in that moment, when you notice your one-upping roommate trying to say all the things you can't do, that's exactly when you sabotage your inner roommate with a more positive suggestion! Or, better yet, just shut your roommate up entirely and empty the thoughts from your mind as you focus on the sensations of your body.

This is also how to succeed at highline slacklining. You know the guys who walk across razor-thin flat pieces of rope, hundreds of feet above a canyon? They are doing this every moment they're up there.

This is also how to succeed at yoga: You overcome your thoughts even when holding a pose that hurts beyond what your brain can comprehend.

Interestingly, this is also how the boys in many rites of passage overcame (and still overcome) the physical pain involved with their ordeals.

Succeed at this challenge and you will see that *you are more than your thoughts and more than your emotions.* Being a man sometimes means having the ability to tell your brain that it's wrong about what it's saying to you. It's having the confidence to tell your own brain, when it doubts what you're capable of, that it needs to shut up and let your true self do the talking.

# YOUR CORE BELIEFS

Let's have a look at Danny Way's core self-beliefs:

**I am not my thoughts.**
**Nothing's too gnarly.**
**I've got this.**

These beliefs don't apply only to skateboarding. Skating is just the tool that Danny used to discover and apply these truths for himself.

But without a Great Wall of China to jump over, how do you start to believe these things?

Well, what if I told you that you have an opportunity to become as hard-core as Danny Way every single day?

Instead of complaining when things go wrong (and they will) or wallowing in the pain when it hurts (again, it will) or burying your face in a video game when something's intimidating (it will be), simply notice what's going on inside your mind and then replace the negative thoughts or feelings with one of your core self-beliefs.

Think about it: It's not that Danny didn't ever wipe out, experience tragedy, or doubt himself. His wipeouts are considered the most painful ever experienced—not just by skateboarders, but by athletes in all board sports! And he's got a life story loaded to the brim with heart-wrenching tragedy.

This means that he's executed what most of us think of as super-human *because of how his mind works*. When he has a negative thought or a moment of pain, he first acknowledges it with some-thing like "Oh yeah, that's a dark thought" or "Wow, that broken ankle hurts." But then he replaces the thought with a better man-tra: "I am not my thoughts. Nothing's too gnarly. I've got this."

The cool thing is that you get to decide what your own core self-beliefs are! But to get started, try replacing your negative be-liefs with Danny's core self-beliefs. Like this:

## INNER ROOMMATE SAYS:

I'm scared that the team we're up against is going to be too much to handle.

I'm not sure I can put up with my teacher/classmate/ little brother another minute.

I'm unsure as to how we'll survive as a species with all the problems in the world.

My panic attacks are overwhelming. This anxiety is crippling.

### BASE CAMP OF BELIEF ANSWERS:

I am not my thoughts.

Nothing's too gnarly.

I've got this.

I'm worried next year's classes are going to be too overwhelming.

I'm afraid of asking my crush to the dance.

What if my friend or family member passes away?

# GATHER YOUR INTEL

In order to successfully and consistently replace the inner roommate nonsense with your core self-beliefs, there are three strategies you can use at any moment to become self-aware. Using these techniques, you'll start to be able to "see" every thought, emotion, and physical sensation you have as separate from yourself, without judging and without reacting. And wouldn't you know it, that's how you buy yourself time to replace your inner roommate's voice with your core self-beliefs. These all take skill, and they take time to get good. But with practice, you're going to be able to hijack your own thoughts and emotions and even your physical sensations, instead of letting them hijack you.

These techniques you're about to get are so powerful that the world-renowned David Lynch Foundation has used them in more than seven hundred inner-city schools across America to help reduce stress and anxiety. The results are pretty spectacular. In the schools in areas with some of the highest crime, dropout, and drug rates in the country, their Quiet Time program has reduced suspensions by 86 percent and violent crimes by 65 percent, and it resulted in a 40 percent decrease in stress, anxiety, and depression. Plus a 10 percent increase in test scores! These work for skateboarding, anxiety, and pop quizzes alike because they're how you become self-aware and get in the zone.

*Okay, get to it, man! What are the three intel strategies?*

## 1. EMOTIONAL INTEL STRATEGY: NAME THE FEELING

There is incredible power in naming your own emotions. It's really as simple as it sounds. By saying, "I feel really angry right now," you take yourself out of the anger that you're feeling. Just by labeling it, you remind yourself that you are not your anger (or helplessness, frustration, fear, anxiety, or any other negative emotion). You are more permanent than the feelings!

After you take a moment to simply give a name to what you're feeling, it's your choice whether to let yourself actually feel the emotion that you have named. Remember, your emotions don't own you. You own your emotions.

## 2. PHYSICAL INTEL STRATEGY: BODY SCAN

Have you ever gone through security at an airport? There's this weird glass chamber they make you step into. You hold your hands above your head and then the machine scans your body to check for weapons. Then someone either sees a good-to-go green light and waves you through, or they're flashed a no-way red light and they stop you to pat you down.

This is kinda like that, except much less creepy. YOU are the person who's analyzing the results of your own body scan. Starting at the top of your noggin, imagine a big flat invisible disc that scans down your body, then tells you about what it finds.

Beginning with your head: Do you have a headache? Are your thoughts whirring? Remember, you're not trying to change anything. You're just observing.

The scanner moves down just a bit. Is it fuzzy in your brain? Is there tension in your chin? What about your neck? Is there pain?

Slowly, over about thirty seconds, the imaginary disc surveys down through your shoulders, chest, belly button, groin, thighs, knees, to your toes.

Your only job is to get a picture of what's going on in your body. By completing this exercise, you develop more self-awareness. Your body doesn't own you. You own your body.

## 3. MENTAL INTEL STRATEGY: WATCHING YOUR BREATH

I've saved the best for last. You've seen Maasai warrior Kakuta Hamisi and legendary skateboarder Danny Way both use this technique and you didn't even realize it. That's because nearly every single human has this ability, but very few of us know how to use it with true skill.

This tool helps puts mountaineers like me on top of Mount Everest, and it was used by free diver Herbert Nitsch to swim to the world-record free diving depth of 702 feet underwater!

Ready for the super secret? It's *watching and controlling your breath.*

Controlling your breath is the key to affecting the things in your body that you can't control: your heartbeat, your blood pressure, your state of mind.

*Mmmmkay,* you might be thinking. *But how does this help with pain management, free diving, emotional support, and climbing mountains?*

Here's how: As you read this sentence, "watch" your breath go in. And watch it go out. Just observe it. You're not trying to change it in any way, okay? All you're trying to do is to "see" your breath. Just watch it.

This is so incredibly powerful because if you have a negative thought, belief, or sensation, and then you shift your attention to your breath, you remind yourself that you aren't owned by that stinkin' roommate in your head! Just by shifting your attention to your breathing, you kick your inner roommate out and plop yourself back down in control of things. You're the person who really belongs there.

Remember, your thoughts don't own you. You own your thoughts.

Everyone can use this technique to overcome great challenges. For example, consider the levels of physical pain that women experience when in labor. Yeah, I'm talking about birthing a child. It comes with excruciating pain, and do you know what many women have used to overcome those labor pains? These same three intel strategies.

**DR. MITHU STORONI** recommends a calming technique called 5-2-7 breathing. Navy SEALs use something very similar when they're under intense pressure. This technique will lower your heart rate, calm your nerves, soothe anxiety, and get you into a state of self-awareness. It's even proven to help you make better decisions! It's great for using before an important test, big speech, competitive game, or anxiety-producing performance.

Each number in the 5-2-7 sequence represents a number of counts. Each count is about one second.

First, you inhale as you count to five. Take all that air in, slow and controlled, as you just watch your lungs expand.

Second, when your lungs are totally full, hold your breath as you count to two.

Finally, exhale super slowly as you count to seven. Just breathe out and, over seven seconds, force all that old and stale air out of your lungs.

**Do that whole breathing sequence at least three times and you're going to notice yourself getting out of your head, into your body, and more calm and confident.**

# GROWING YOUR INFINITY MUSCLES

Have you ever noticed how everybody thinks something is impossible until someone does it? Then suddenly tons of people start doing the thing that everybody previously thought was "impossible," right? That's how it was with Roger Bannister, the first guy to run a mile in under four minutes. Now? Lots of people do that. That's also how it was with Greta Thunberg, the climate activist who was told she'd never be able to make a difference. Now? Millions have joined her war cry and rallied in protection of our Earth.

Each of these Warriors was told "It's not possible." Then they searched themselves for what *they* deemed possible, not what *the voices running amok in their heads* deemed possible. Each of them learned to go within, to dig up persistence when their brains said they couldn't give any more.

You can also prove your own superhuman powers by becoming self-aware. Your true self is infinite. Whenever you dig deep to find your inner strength, you gain more abilities to dig even deeper.

Then, when the next challenge arises, the old stuff that once felt hard suddenly seems easy. Building infinity muscles is a lot like building physical muscles!

The whole process?

1. First, use your three self-awareness intel strategies to get yourself in the zone. Remember them? Here's your cheat sheet: Name the feeling, complete a body scan, and watch your breath.

2. Once you're in the zone, replace your negative thoughts with better beliefs.

And . . . don't forget to call it quits when you need to. Take time to rest, play, and recover. That last one is really important. Nobody becomes a total rock star right out of the gate.

When guys get it in their heads that they have to push through their pain—inner or physical—they put themselves in danger of injury. Or burnout.

This is why, after you've done steps 1 and 2, if the negative sensation or feeling returns, it's so important to give yourself permission to call it quits. Get some sleep, go play, take a break, rest up, and come back fresh. The battle will still be there to be fought on another day.

We say in climbing that "the mountain will still be there tomorrow." Look, nobody makes it up every mountain every time—it's only the climbers who are able to rest and recover who live to climb another day. Danny is the same: he frequently takes long breaks to either heal from his injuries or regain his stoke for skating.

Pushing your limits is an incredible thing *when the time is right to do so.* This is not about pushing through pain; this is about self-awareness, which also means knowing when to stop, rest, and recover. Or not attempting something at all! Using the three self-intel strategies every day will help you to get better at quickly identifying the right moments for each.

There you have it! That's the whole process that will make you superhuman (over time). This is how you build infinity muscles of self-awareness. That's how you get in the zone, become superhuman like Danny Way, and accomplish the "impossible."

You have passed Challenge 2! Congrats! Plus, Challenge 3 is officially unlocked. Great job on your progress, Warrior, you're showing massive promise.

# TRAINING GROUNDS:
## BECOME SELF-AWARE

### KNOW IT

Boys live in constant reaction to their emotions, bodies, and thoughts. True Warriors consciously choose their self-beliefs.

### ACT ON IT

☐ Right now, practice all three self-awareness intel strategies: Name the emotions you're feeling. Do a body scan, from head to toe, over thirty seconds, to "see" what your body feels like. And watch your breath. Now you're in control!

☐ When you do these things, take note of all the mental chatter going on in your head. Remember, you're not trying to change anything. You're just observing the thoughts.

☐ With the negative thoughts you see, do some roommate sabotage! Replace those thoughts with positive self-beliefs. Try starting with *I am not my thoughts. Nothing's too gnarly. I've got this.* Or decide on a set of beliefs that are more true to you!

# CHALLENGE 3:
# SHIFT YOUR FINISH LINE

Being a man has very little to do with trying to be a man, and a lot to do with being present and trustworthy, grounded and transparent, and showing up as a warrior of integrity and intimacy, compassionately cutting through the roots of whatever is obstructing one's well-being.

—ROBERT AUGUSTUS MASTERS,
*TO BE A MAN: A TRUE GUIDE TO MASCULINE POWER*

# FROM DUST TO GLORY

Your helmet lens is completely covered with filth and grime. The dust in the air is so thick, there are only two things you're able to see: the hood of your 1969 Volkswagen Beetle and the faint glow of the flashing yellow safety light mounted on the vehicle in front of you.

*How am I supposed to navigate if I can't even see the track?!*

To be fair, you've got it easy—you just have to call out what your military-grade GPS unit is telling you. Your driver, Nick, on the other hand, has to steer the car! He pegs the gas pedal to the floor, and your 1600cc motor screams like an angry banshee as it sucks dirt into the carburetor. The oil temp gauge redlines. The smells of burning engine parts whip through the windows and into your dust-clogged nostrils. "Bochito can handle it!" you say, calling your beloved black-and-green Volkswagen Bug by the racing-industry nickname for cars in its class. "Keep tailing that car!"

The dust cloud consumes everything. The *polvo,* as it's called in Spanish, is everywhere. It's in your helmet, your eyelids, your impact vest. It's covering your black hair and coating your tanned skin. Because this race takes place over several days, your team trades shifts to cover the mileage. At the start of each of yours, you can barely buckle your seat belt because it's so clogged with grime.

You're racing in the longest, toughest, most grueling off-road race in the world. It's the sport-defining annual event called the Baja 1000. For off-road racing fans, it's the Super Bowl, the Stanley Cup, and Mardi Gras all rolled into one. But for racers like you, it means traveling at cheetah-like speeds through an obstacle course of death traps and dirt for three days straight.

Your suspension and tires are getting worked by every rock and pothole in Baja California, Mexico. You feel like a human bobble-head as your helmet-encased skull whacks against the roll netting in your window . . . again and again. But every time you remember what you're racing for, you know it's all gonna be worth it.

Because while the literal finish line of the Baja 1000 may be in the beach town of La Paz, Mexico, your true finish line is Ensenada. In that town there's a shelter and a school called Casa Esperanza. *The House of Hope.* It's a safe haven and rehabilitation center that helps battered and abused mothers and their children get back on their feet.

All over your off-road racing machine are the handprints of the kids who live at Casa Esperanza. Before any race Bochito's in, every child gets to dip their hands in neon paint—they choose the color—and press their paint-covered hands against Bochito. The hands symbolize those kids pushing Bochito along. Every inch of every mile of every race.

And, right about now, you could certainly use that extra push. Because if Nick slows down in the slightest, sand will overtake Bo-chito's wheels and that'll be game over. You'll be stuck, entrenched in the dried silt. Or, at any minute—any second—Nick could take a sharp turn and send you down an arroyo, straight into a cactus, or through a booby trap set by rogue locals. *You shouldn't be doing this,* your brain says. But then you hear your mouth say, "Dude, stay on it! Don't let 'em go!"

Nick takes his job seriously and is driving flawlessly. You look at your GPS and see how far you've come in two days: 1,102 miles. You have no windshield, so you point in the correct direction through the space where it would be. You cheer Nick and Bochito on. "Only 172 miles to go!"

That's when it hits you: *We might just make the finish line!*

In last year's race, you broke down at mile marker 67. For this race, you said you'd be happy logging 500 miles. But now, Bochito is the only remaining vehicle in his class. The other Beetles have smashed into rocks bigger than tanks. They've rolled, wrecked their shocks, overheated, blown tires, or fallen prey to any number of other calamities. Point is, they're all behind you. Now you're racing alongside ATVs, TUTVs, premium motocross bikes, and Humvees. You overtake the 40hp dirt bikes, and 900hp monster trucks overtake you, everyone kicking dust into the Baja California Peninsula's sky.

Bochito is an off-road racing veteran, kitted out with lifted tires for superior ground clearance and cargo netting strapped to the windows to stop you and your driver from flying out. He even rolled a few hundred miles back. But you and your team managed to flip him right side up, make a few repairs, and get him moving. Again. Only problem? Your front right shock is completely gone. Because of that, each left turn puts your head inches from the ground as rocks and dirt shred against Bochito's passenger door.

*C'mon, buddy, hang in there. Just a few miles to go. The kids are gonna love hearing about this!*

You've got to stay vigilant. Locals have laid out strips of tire spikes throughout the desert. There are tractor-sized holes dug up

in the center of the track and covered with palm leaves. Course arrows have been flipped around and made to point in the wrong direction. Ramps have been built to launch unsuspecting vehicles straight into cliff sides, sometimes even causing fatalities.

The track is designed fresh each year, and this is the longest, hardest Baja 1000 . . . ever. Not only is the course 274 miles longer than it's supposed to be, but the booby traps are worse than they've ever been. As you inhale the endless dirt, you say to Nick over the engine's roar, "You know what? We're the only vehicle in our class that's still racing. So let's forget about the trophy. That's not what we're here for. If we can get to the finish line, that'll be enough!"

You're happily watching the miles count down. You see mile marker 1,264. *Ten miles to go!* You even start rehearsing your victory speech.

But the race planners had one last trick up their sleeves.

Suddenly, you see . . . nothing.

No ground. No cactus. No dust. Just air. Your RPMs redline and your engine screams as your wheels spin in the air. *We're . . . we're airborne!*

Midflight, you realize what's happened. You've accidentally launched over *Las Filas.*

The race organizers cut out a dirt staircase cascading down the back of one of the final hills. Each step is over two feet tall.

You're in a Volkswagen Beetle, not an airplane. Bochito anvils from the sky and his underbelly smashes into the corner of a step. You cringe, trying not to imagine the damage. The Beetle grinds, clanks, crunches, scrapes, and bangs against each and every remaining step. Pieces of metal are flying out of Bochito's . . . everywhere. *How could they do this to us? We've nearly finished!*

Your beloved racing car practically crumples as it tumbles down the staircase. You brace yourself, wondering if Bochito will roll.

But then the track flattens! You're in the clear!

With increasing intensity, Nick says to you: "We've got a problem. Something's not right. I can't steer!"

You unbuckle your seat belt and crawl through the hole where the windshield would normally be. With your chest on the hood and your legs bracing your weight inside the cab, you dangle your head to survey the damage. You can hardly believe what you're looking at. As you're trying to comprehend what you're seeing, you say your thoughts out loud, "Nick! The tire . . ."

"What about it?" he demands, gripping the steering wheel.

"It's . . . it's gone! It's somewhere behind us!" Not only the tire, but every part of the assembly that keeps the tire attached is also missing!

Nick says, "But we're going forty miles per hour! What do I do?"

Your reply bleeds out of your face before you can consider the repercussions: "Just keep driving! And lean back!"

You're gonna balance on a motorized tricycle for the remaining four miles to the finish line!

After a mile, you're amazed that it's actually working. But then comes a hill. It's too steep! Bochito chokes and sputters to a stop. The clock is ticking.

Moments later, your chase vehicle shows up. The support team hustles to create a makeshift wheel assembly, and they attach a spare tire to it. You and Nick are each patted on the back, and you're on your way. Bochito crawls up and over the final hill. You spot the finish line. Bochito growls across it and gets a checkered-flag finish.

You look at the official race clock. You're too late. By an hour. You're given a DNF—Did Not Finish.

Stepping out of the passenger seat, you're unrecognizable through the mud and dirt caked onto your hair, your clothes, your skin. You and Nick hug, your helmets dangling in your hands behind each other's backs. For a moment you feel a twinge of regret. The sting of defeat. *We were so close!*

You look at Bochito. He's tattered and broken. Under the silt, you see his classic black paint job and neon-green accents. Then your eyes are drawn to your favorite feature. *The handprints.* Bright red, yellow, pink, orange, and blue evidence of dozens of tiny human hands pressed onto Bochito. You press your hand against one, your fingers so much larger than the print of the child. Your eyes get teary as you smile. You remember your real finish line.

# DENNIS HOLLENBECK: REDEFINING VICTORY

"Those kids are our motivation," says True Warrior Dennis Hollenbeck. He's the real-life navigator in that story. "To those kids," he says, "Bochito is like a living, breathing friend."

What Dennis and Nick didn't realize (as their team scrambled to attach a new tire after their crash down Las Filas) was that thousands of people on the internet were logged in, watching the live-tracking race radar, and *losing their minds.* A tiny blip on the race map was sitting dead still, only a couple of miles from the finish line. Everybody was asking, "Who's this car, #1121?!" The clock was ticking down while the chat forums exploded with everybody trying to figure out whose team #1121 belonged to!

When they finally found out that it was Bochito's transponder, people started Googling and reverse-engineered Bochito's connection to Casa Esperanza. And when everybody saw that they didn't cross the finish line in time, publicity and donations for Casa Esperanza began to pour in! Nick and Dennis, without even knowing about the online buzz, had succeeded at the real reason they race: raising awareness about the kids, fund-raising, generating hope, and bringing awareness to their faith.

A stock 1969 Volkswagen Beetle has absolutely no business racing the dirt roads of Baja California, Mexico. It's an impossible vehicle for the world's toughest motorized off-road adventure race. And that's precisely why Hollenbeck races with it. It proves to those kids that they, too, can overcome impossible odds.

Did Hollenbeck want to finish the Baja 1000 on time? Yeah, of course! But as tempting as it was to define his success by standing on a podium as the sole finisher in his class, he and his H12:One team know that they succeeded at the *real* race. Crazily enough, had Bochito NOT busted his wheel and crossed the race's finish line on time, Hollenbeck's team probably wouldn't have raised the same level of support for the shelter.

Hollenbeck describes racing Bochito like this: "You may not be able to see out of your windshield, but in that moment, you can picture those kids waving their hands through the classroom windows. You might not be able to hear anything over the screaming of your engine, but in your imagination, you hear their rhythmic chanting as you drive their beloved car back home. 'Bo-chi-to! Bo-chi-to! Bo-chi-to!'"

*That* moment is Hollenbeck's TRUE finish line, when the kids see themselves in Bochito. When those kids first arrived at Casa Esperanza, they were missing pieces of their lives. They had been through unthinkable circumstances. But after seeing Bochito nearly destroyed in a race and then repaired and buffed to a shine, with his engine roaring, they start to believe they can be made better than before, too. That's why they never ask, "Did Bochito win?" Instead they ask, "How *is* Bochito?" Which is really their way of asking, "Am I going to be okay, too, after what's happened to me?"

Here's why this matters to you: Crossing other people's finish lines is not a worthwhile goal for your life. Life is not about being the fastest or the richest, or having the most followers. Can those things be fun and awesome hobbies? Of course! But they're not the true finish line, and racing toward them only results in comparison and judgment. Define success by those things and you will never feel peace, contentment, or consistent happiness.

True Warriors measure their success by the values that they choose to live by, not by the speed of their truck (so to speak). Real success is about HOW you race and what you drive TOWARD. Part of being a Warrior means recognizing that false finish lines don't bring long-term happiness. When True Warriors recognize the hollow sound of victory, they shift gears and make a conscious, dedicated decision to race toward a better finish line for their lives.

**Challenge 3 is to shift your finish line away from what society tells you it should be. Instead, define your finish line by your personally chosen set of values. You will succeed at this challenge once you've created a statement of those values—it's called your Warrior Creed, and you're gonna make it, right here in this challenge.**

Let's get to it. . . .

# WHAT MAKES YOU WORTHY

Do you know the legend of Thor's hammer? Yeah, like from Norse mythology and the Marvel movies.

The hammer's named Mjölnir, and everyone knows it's the most powerful weapon in the universe. Thor's father, Odin, enchanted it by saying, "Whosoever holds this hammer, if he be worthy, shall possess the power of Thor."

Anyone can see the legendary weapon sitting *right there,* but Odin's spell prevents you from picking it up, let alone taking a swing with it—unless you're worthy.

Okay, so the natural question is . . . how do you become worthy? (In other words, why did it take Captain America twenty-one separate films before he was finally able to fight with it in *Avengers: Endgame*? It's because he rode his motorbike without a helmet, disqualifying him from true worthiness. *Kidding!*)

I did some research to find the actual answer. And I kinda went deep.

The leading theory is that Captain America had character all along but was still a Blood Knight at heart. Meaning he defined himself solely by his ability to fight and valued his role as a soldier more than he valued anything else. When it finally clicked for the Cap, the mighty hammer Mjölnir deemed him worthy because he decided to fight with humility, courage, and life-defending values for the greater good of the war.

So what makes YOU worthy? What is a real-life, hammer-worthy finish line in our culture? More important, which character traits do you have that make *you* hammer-worthy?

As I've said, measuring your success by other people's standards is a formula for constant comparison and anxiety. Your worth doesn't lie in the height of the mountains you climb (and that's coming from a guy who has climbed the tallest ones on the planet).

You will constantly feel like you are not enough if you chase status, chase fame, or try to outperform other people. Don't misunderstand: Everyone needs to be passionate about what they do. We all need a thing. Off-road racing is something Dennis Hollenbeck loves. If your thing happens to get you a lot of likes, money, or fame, then that's awesome, and you can use your influence for a whole lot of good. But if you measure your worth as a person *based* on those things, then mark my words, you will become a miserable sack of a human.

True Warriors all pretty much agree on the most hammer-worthy of all finish lines: It's living by your values.

That's why the good guys ARE *the good guys* in movies! We root for them because they fight to defend their values and their tribes.

Right now, I'm challenging you to look within and define your values. What's your true finish line in life?

Your task is to choose the top five life values that are most true to you. You can use the list that follows for inspiration. These could be values you already have, like the ones your family has passed down to you. More important than anything, *we're looking for the ones you believe are most important for a man to live by.* Approach this task with radical honesty and total self-awareness!

(BTW, radical honesty is a step up from run-of-the-mill honesty. It means to be 100 percent truthful, telling and acknowledging the *full* truth in all situations. White lies and partial truths aren't worth it; even if your truth could cause others pain, and even if something is hard to admit, being radically honest creates far less hurt and anxiety for yourself in the end—and it's just the right thing to do.)

This is a critical step, so pick the ones that are most authentic to you! Which of these are most authentic to *your* life's *real* finish line? Do you want to be . . .

- Radically Honest
- Reliable
- Loyal
- Open-minded
- Cheerful
- Optimistic
- Faithful
- Organized
- Environmentally conscious
- Present
- Accepting
- Hopeful
- Dedicated
- Creative
- Kind
- Good humored
- Compassionate

- Adventurous
- Ambitious
- Passionate
- Respectful
- Self-loving
- Brave
- Patriotic
- Committed
- Generous
- Thoughtful
- Nurturing
- Humble
- Serving
- Tender
- Spiritual
- Motivated
- Courageous

Personally, my top values are: presence, radical honesty, compassion, courage, and environmental consciousness.

What about you? Would you be stoked if, in eighty years, you somehow heard people talking about you at your own funeral and they said you'd embodied those five values? If not, which would you prefer? The ones you settle on should make you the good kind of proud. After all, this is your definition of what it means for you to have a life worth living.

# YOUR INTERNAL GPS

Like Nick, you are the driver of your life. But like Hollenbeck, you are *also* the navigator. His most valuable piece of equipment when navigating is that military-grade, premium GPS unit. Your own internal GPS needs to be able to tell you where to turn and course correct when you get off track, right?

In your life, that's your *integrity.* Your sense of integrity will tell you when you're starting to veer off track from your values. Integrity is telling the same story no matter who you're talking to. It's doing the same thing whether your buddies are watching, your teacher is watching, your mother is watching, or nobody is watching. Integrity is having nothing to hide because you're always the same person, no matter who you're with or where you are. Whatever real men say to their buddies, they also say to women in the room. They're the same person no matter who is around.

The true test of integrity is asking yourself, "Would I be embarrassed if anyone knew the full truth about my actions right now?" or "Would I honestly care if some other person on the planet heard what I'm saying out loud right now?"

Every one of us can act like a jerk sometimes. We mess up. We forget. We are late. We break stuff. We make mistakes. We hurt people. Heroes are those who handle these crashes well. For you, that means when you mess up, you own it. You learn from it. You apologize. You make it right. And you learn from your mistakes so that you don't launch yourself off Las Filas (or make the same mistake) again. The real skill isn't in never taking a wrong turn. Rather, it's in seeing how quickly you can recognize it when you're off track . . . and then course correct.

# YOUR WARRIOR CREED

What if you started driving and your phone's GPS randomly started screaming at you? "Oh my gosh, look, there's a street right there!" "Hey, whaddya think is down that road? You could make a U-turn here. But prolly not." "SHOE STORE! THERE'S A SHOE STORE!"

It would frustrate the heck out of you, right?

You know who it would remind me of? Your inner roommate! Yeah, that dude's back for revenge. And this time, he's trying to take you down paths that will distract you from your values. He's setting up booby traps to derail you from your true finish line. With him shooting off at the mouth, trying to get you to go down one-way streets, make obviously wrong turns, and distract you from your values, you as a Warrior need a clear, easy-to-memorize set of directions that will guide you, turn by turn, to your final destination.

That's why, in this section, you're going to create your very own Warrior Creed.

Here's how: We're going to take some lessons from the Special

Operations Forces of the US military. These guys are the best of the best, and they have to be tough as nails. They're lethal. They're humble. They're the dudes who get the job done and don't expect thanks for being the best there is. It's even part of the Special Forces Creed that they "serve quietly, not seeking recognition or accolades."

My friend Steve Hemmann is a West Point graduate. He was a US Army Special Forces Soldier (aka the Green Berets), and he also went through Ranger school. When I asked him what he thinks makes him a man, he shared that many military units have special mottos or creeds that each team member must memorize—then try to live up to.

Green Berets, for example, have a motto, "De Oppresso Liber," which is Latin for "to free the oppressed." I mean, how epic would you feel if you had your own Latin motto?

"Okay, what's the creed you had to memorize?" I asked.

The moment he opened his mouth to answer, everything about his demeanor changed. He stood up straight. He faced me and leaned in and looked me dead in the eye. I could imagine the strength of an entire platoon of soldiers standing behind him in unison.

By heart, verbatim, he said, "Acknowledging the fact that a Ranger is a more elite soldier who arrives at the cutting edge of battle by land, sea, or air, I accept the fact that as a Ranger, my country expects me to move further, faster, and fight harder than any other soldier. . . ."

He continued until he had recited all remaining six stanzas of the Ranger Creed. He wasn't bragging. And he wasn't being shy. He was radically honest, laying bare a creed that he aspires to live by, as a man. And I was floored.

When Steve told me the Ranger Creed, I started thinking . . . *Do I have something like this? Something I believe in so deeply that it transforms my posture from standard issue to imposing strength?*

I couldn't say I did. So I made one.

And now you are going to do the same. You're going to create a personal creed that deeply resonates with you.

Your Warrior Creed is your life's GPS. When your mud-caked helmet visor makes it impossible to see the way, your creed gives you direction. It's a statement that defines the values you live by. It guides you and defines you. It tells you where to turn and reminds you when you've gone off track.

Here's the good news that makes this easy: Your Warrior Creed is already in you. If you were radically honest when you chose your top five values, then you already know the truth about the kind of man you *really* want to be. Now you've just got to write it down.

More good news for you: Over half of your creed is already written! No joke—you already have three of the five parts.

Remember when you decided to Step Up in Challenge 1? You can boil that down to: *I commit to know, own, and act on everything I can do to become my best self and protect my tribe.*

Part two you already have as well! Remember when you became self-aware and replaced your negative beliefs from Challenge 2? That's *I am not my thoughts. Nothing's too gnarly, and whatever the challenge, I've got this.*

And wouldn't you know it? You just picked up the next part of your creed right here in Challenge 3. That's *While I'm not always perfect, I trust my sense of integrity to guide me perfectly in my pursuit of the following traits.*

Next, go ahead and write a single paragraph that summarizes

your values, or just list the values—what's important is that the words of your Warrior Creed move you. You want to be so proud of what's in it that, when you recite it, you feel it resonate deep in your gut. Maybe you even get chills on your neck. Maybe you lift your chin and roll your shoulders back. You should, because your Warrior Creed is your own definition of YOU.

Your Warrior Creed is how you say, "This is who I am, what I stand for, what I believe in, and what I'm here for," as though you are your own branch of elite special forces!

Here's my entire personal Warrior Creed:

*I aspire to know, own, and act on everything I can to become my best self and protect my tribe. I choose to step up and live my life in a way that makes me proud of who I am.*

*I am not my thoughts. Nothing's too gnarly. Whatever the challenge, I've got this.*

*Each day, I act with courage to leave the world better than I found it. I live in the now, hopeful for the future and accepting of my past, and I treat myself and the people I love with radical honesty, compassion, and humor. I'm as rugged as I am classy. As shrewd as I am kind.*

*While I'm not always perfect, I trust my sense of integrity to guide me perfectly in my pursuit of these traits.*

That's it. To me, that's a pretty stellar life.

But what's a stellar life for *you*?

It's totally legit to adopt a creed from an organization you're a part of. Or from clubs in your school like Future Business Leaders of America, Future Farmers of America, 4-H, or Family, Career, and Community Leaders of America, which have creeds of their own. Enter virtually any church, mosque, synagogue, or temple, and you'll see people who value their creeds and recite them as they worship. You can take inspiration (or borrow a creed, if it's true to you!) from anywhere.

However you find yours, you will succeed at this challenge by writing out your own Warrior Creed. After you've written it out, put it on your bathroom mirror, in your backpack or wallet, or beside your bed. Commit to memorizing it. Follow it. Do so, and you can have 100 percent confidence that you will always have guideposts to help you find your way.

Remember, it doesn't have to be perfect, but you gotta start somewhere. So begin creating your creed already!

# TRAINING GROUNDS:
## SHIFT YOUR FINISH LINE

### KNOW IT

Boys race toward the finish lines that others have chosen. True Warriors define their life finish lines by the values chosen in each of their personal Warrior Creeds!

### ACT ON IT

☐ Think of a moment when you were chasing after a goal that wasn't really your own, and it wasn't very fun or fulfilling to pursue. Got it? Good! Now remember that feeling so that you can recognize it in the future! Whenever you feel it again, you will know it's time to shift your finish line!

☐ Choose the five values that resonate most with what kind of Warrior you aspire to be. Use the list on page 69 for inspiration, but by all means, choose your own if needed!

☐ Write out your complete Warrior Creed. A creed is the mark of elite soldiers from around the world, so memorize yours and let it guide your actions!

# ACHIEVEMENT UNLOCKED! LEVEL I COMPLETE!

Sometimes you must hurt in order to know,
fall in order to grow, lose in order to gain,
because most of life's greatest lessons
are learned through pain.

—*NARUTO SHIPPUDEN,*
ANIMATED SERIES ABOUT A BOY BECOMING
THE GREATEST NINJA IN JAPAN

# CONGRATULATIONS, MASTER OF WARRIOR WEAPONRY!

You did it! You've mastered the weapons that warriors use. Look at you go, home slice! It's my honor and duty, as your Warrior Guide, to designate you as a member of the War Council.

You've now got a seriously solid foundation for being self-sufficient. Just think back to when you were a wee aspiring Warrior: First you stepped up as a man in your face-off against a legit Maasai warrior. Then you became self-aware and launched yourself over the Great Wall of China. Finally you shifted your finish line to shred off-road for 1,274 miles through the Baja California Peninsula. Pretty rad human you've become, if you ask me!

But you're not a Warrior yet. Phase II of your training is about mastering your defenses. In the next three challenges, you're going to secure your base camp's perimeter, form your Battle Crew, and learn how to hold down the fort at all costs.

In other words: Learn to protect your tribe and the values that you stand for.

# YOUR WARRIOR GUIDE'S BATTLE

Now that you're a ranking member of the Warrior class, you've earned the right to some details about why I was chosen as your Warrior Guide. And to make the point best, let's look at how Warrior Guides were selected in ancient cultures.

Put yourself in the shoes of a real-life thirteen-year-old boy undergoing an ancient rite of passage. Can you imagine having your finger cut off like the kids of the Native American Mandan tribe? Or having to go away for months to hunt for your own food and scavenge water from springs? Or being injected with a poison that makes you delirious for two days? Those were just some of the wake-up calls aimed to teach boys that there are real and legitimate threats to them and their tribes. In those cases, their guides were preparing them to defend against the worst possible threats they'd face.

If the guide failed? The kid died. He'd be eaten or killed by enemies. Sometimes both.

These days? The threats aren't bullet ants. They're mental health problems. Destruction of the environment. Inhumane treatment of people due to gender, race, religion, or sexuality. Bullying. Attacks on our schools. And those are just a few of the many Kings of Beasts we've gotta take down.

And me? I was chosen as your Warrior Guide because I have experienced some brutal traumas. But before we go there, you need to understand what that means for you. I'm not telling you my personal stories for your entertainment—this is for when something brutal happens to you, too.

In today's world, at some point, we all experience what I call "wake-up smacks." Maybe it's already happened to you. Maybe it hasn't happened yet. Maybe it feels like it keeps happening. Maybe it won't happen to you for a while. But at some point, you will run headlong into a moment in your life that feels core shaking. An I'm-not-the-same-after-that kind of moment. It's like we somehow need one of these wake-up smacks because it makes us look around and truly recognize that there's *really* precious stuff in this world that is worth defending.

Plus, the moment you are suddenly forced to deal with traumatic stuff—and there is a one billion percent chance that you will—you will be defined by how you face it. *Men are made in how we heal.*

See, I'm your Warrior Guide not just because something traumatic happened to me. I'm your Warrior Guide because, with a lot of help and guidance, I learned how to *heal well* after something traumatic happened to me. At my core, I'm now a better human being. When you, in your own life, are suddenly forced to deal with that something brutal—this Warrior training stuff is what sets you up to come back stronger than ever.

*So, what happened?*

A few years ago, I was in Cape Town, South Africa, and was scheduled to deliver an epic TEDx speech. Have you ever seen the videos of speakers delivering a talk while standing on a red circle? On this particular day, that was gonna be me.

I was ready to roll. My fully memorized speech was about climbing the world's tallest mountain, Mount Everest. The plan was to crush it onstage and prove my mountain-man toughness to the world. I even had slides and videos scored to heart-tugging mood music.

Except, on the morning of the talk, I saw a dead body in the shower.

It was as sudden and out of nowhere as that sentence. Imagine it happening to you: You're shampooing your hair, warm suds are running down your face, and when you open your eyes, your feet are trapped in a block of frozen shower water along with a bluish corpse.

Gruesome, right? I was so startled by the vision that I jumped back, slipped, and fell over, cracking my head. Seeing stars, I thought, *That was freakin' weird.*

Immediately, I knew who I'd seen in my hallucination. His name was Mohammed. On my ascent up Mount Everest, on summit night, I was next to him when he took his last breath. His team had already left him for dead and he was frozen into the ice. I'd desperately wanted to give him medicine, to start a rescue effort. But he took his last breath within seconds of when I encountered him. And my guide convinced me that a retrieval effort for a dead man would have endangered me and everyone on the mountain. I stayed beside his body as long as I could, saying prayers for him in every religion I could think of, hoping one might have matched his beliefs. But the negative-thirty-eight-degree temperatures and twenty-mile-per-hour wind gusts at 28,000 feet above sea level are a deadly combination. Ice pellets were whipping my face, and my tank of oxygen was leaking. It's called the Death Zone because, sooner or later, if you spend long enough there, you will die no matter who you are. I had to keep moving to generate body heat, or I would die, too. So I continued up the mountain.

That was Mohammed. That's who was frozen in the shower with me. For months since returning from the Himalayas, I'd been having night terrors about that entire ordeal. Except I kept dreaming that it was me who was frozen into the ice.

Back in the shower, on the morning of my TEDx talk, I told myself to toughen up as I crawled from the tub. *Don't tell anyone. It's shameful.* It was like I had a song on repeat that was saying over and over that I had to man up and prove myself at all costs. *Never admit to or reveal weakness. Don't talk about what hurts inside. Don't even acknowledge it's there. Push through the pain; plaster a smile on your face and show how tough you are. Pain doesn't even register for me.*

The kind of shame that I experienced after not being able to help Mohammed was toxic. Toxic shame doesn't just say, "I'm embarrassed because I did something bad." Instead, toxic shame says, "I *am* bad, at my core." It convinced me that because I wasn't able to save Mohammed, I was responsible for his death.

Have you ever felt toxic shame? I'm not talking about encountering a body. I'm asking if you've ever experienced something that makes you feel like you *are* bad, that everything is your fault, and that something has been permanently ruined *because of you*? If yes, that's what toxic shame looks like. I'm right there with you. And so are many, many other guys.

With "be tough, dude" as the jacked-up creed I was living by, I pulled myself off the bathroom floor and checked to see if my head was bleeding. No blood. I brushed it off.

Eventually, I got dressed and went to a café, trying to shake off seeing Mohammed in the shower. I was shocked when I could barely hand cash across the counter because I was trembling so badly. I was shaking with an inexplicable sense of dread that I was going to be attacked. *Stabbed.*

I went numb, operating on autopilot, and before I really knew what was happening, I was onstage, delivering my speech. The big TEDx talk! Two hundred people in front of me, cameras, photographers, potentially millions of viewers online over time, bright lights!

I've given a lot of speeches in my life. I've been paid to speak in forty-eight states and seven countries, so I know stage fright. But this? This was different. It was as though the audience could all somehow see that I was too slow, too weak, to save someone's life.

It was a panicked feeling of *I'm not good enough, I'll never be good enough, and everyone out there can see that I am not enough.* As I continued the speech, I could hardly catch my breath—suddenly, I was having flashbacks to other traumatic life moments. Like the time my oxygen ran out on Everest, and the time I was held against the lockers by my throat in middle school.

I told the TEDx audience all the cool stuff about Everest, and I put on the show I thought they wanted. Only when I got offstage, I was covered in sweat. Drenched.

My friend Sandra, who was at the speech, noticed and thankfully knew how to connect with me *with heart*. See, she was further along in her Warrior training. It was a few days later when she said, "In most instances, if someone broke their leg, and they kept walking around on it but kept saying they were fine—what would you tell them?"

"I'd tell them they need to see a doctor," I said flatly.

"Yeah, but this person is trying to be tough. They claim they don't ever need help and they pride themselves on gritting through the pain and—"

"I'd say they're being prideful and nobody's impressed," I interrupted. "They should find a really good doctor to put the bone back in place."

That's when Sandra flipped it back on me (like a good friend will): "Yeah, exactly. It's your own advice—so take it. You are walking around telling yourself 'It's fine' when it's not. Heaps of doctors know how to put your heart back in place."

I tried to save face, hold it together, suck it up. I basically repeated the same phony lines to her that I'd been telling myself all along: "I climb the world's tallest mountains. People fly me all over the world to hear what I have to say. I'm tough. I don't need help." I'd gotten so good at hiding that I was terrified to finally face the truth, pain, and darkness head-on. I was terrified to pick my spear up off the floor. But Sandra handed it back to me and told me to use it.

If I had any hope of healing, there was no way out of the pain except through it. There's a quote Winston Churchill may have said, though it's been attributed to a couple of sources. It applied to me then, and perhaps will apply to you today: "If you're going through hell, keep going."

# MEN AND INNER PAIN

Truth is, at some point, every single human on the planet experiences inner pain of some kind. I don't know what you're going through right now, or what you've gone through in the past. But I know for sure that, if you're human, there's something in your life that hurts. Whatever your thing is, it sucks. And you are not alone.

Statistics show that more and more guys are feeling more and more isolated. We may even feel like the pain is permanent. And we're losing our brothers because of it. Here's proof: among fifteen- to nineteen-year-olds, the suicide rate in the United States has increased by 47 percent since the year 2000. The *Journal of the American Medical Association* says it's the second leading cause of death in this age group. And of those suicides, do you know what percentage of them are boys? It's 78 percent. Yeah, over three in four teens who die by suicide are boys.

That's tragic, and it has to stop. These aren't random, faceless kids. They had families, teams, teachers, pets, and crushes. It's

screwed up because not one of those suicides—not a single one—
had to happen.

According to an article in *Men's Health,* "More than 3 million
men struggle with anxiety daily. . . . An estimated 10 million men in
the U.S. will suffer from an eating disorder in their lifetime. . . . One
out of every five men will develop an alcohol dependency during
his life."

If you feel sadness for what you're reading here, it's proof that
you're not alone. Everybody, men and women alike, is in this together. And we have the power to change this by simply beginning
to admit that we feel pain. That's how hope starts. That's also how
guys can start to change these tragic statistics. If we stop ignoring
it, if we stop being ashamed of it, then we will learn to deal with
our pain in constructive ways.

That might sound scary, so I'll go first and share another story
that was very painful.

A very close friend of mine died when I was fifteen years old.
Three days after the car accident that killed him, I went to my school
counselor. I was in tears, looking for some relief, some help, some
comfort, some . . . oh, I don't know . . . counseling?!

His response was to throw up his hands and say, "I don't know
what to tell you here. It's just one of those things you've got to
tough out. You're gonna have to get over it and move on."

It was the right choice to speak up to an adult in this situation.
And luckily, many school counselors are awesome. But that guy
should have been fired. Seriously.

I went back to class bewildered and still crying. My classmates
laughed at me. As I slumped into my desk chair, the kid sitting behind me stabbed me in the back with a sharpened pencil and told
me to "quit being a little bitch."

I went to the teacher with blood running down my back. The teacher didn't look up and only said, "Class, please keep your hands and pencils to yourselves."

This taught me to suck it up, to numb my pain. I had received the all-too-common message that, if I ever reveal what's really going on, it will result in shame and betrayal. In this case, that message came in the form of being literally stabbed in the back.

From where I sit now, I know that the kid who stabbed me was a hurt kid. And realistically, it was a hurt counselor and a hurt teacher. Hurt people hurt people, after all. But back then, when the shame had nowhere to go except inside, I became really, really depressed.

I bet this is not a new or unusual story to you. Sure, the details of your own version may differ, but I'd wager a thousand bucks that, if you're being honest, you've experienced this same kind of suffering in silence; you've experienced something painful and felt like you had to bottle it up.

As guys, we are taught that we have three options for how to deal with stuff like this:

1. Numb it gone.
2. Tough it out.
3. Be nice.

Only problem? All three of those choices are completely destructive. Not only to the person doing these things with their pain, but to everyone around them, too.

Some people have panic attacks. Some develop addictions. Some try to choke other kids against lockers. Some let it out on the sports field. Some become abusive. Some let themselves be treated like doormats. Some bury themselves in studies. And some, like me, get depressed.

We are all a part of this cycle of hurt. We have to choose to live better. Fortunately, I had a strong support system of people who taught me to assemble my warrior armor. Now that your weapons mastery training is complete, I'm going to do the same for you.

It's time for the next phase of your training. Together, we're going to upgrade your line of defenses. Get ready to level up your armor, you awesome Warrior apprentice, you!

# WAY OF THE WARRIOR

My single favorite video game of all time is one of the *Final Fantasy* games. In this particular story, you play a Dark Knight who has to climb a mountain to battle "a great enemy." But when you arrive at the top, your rival is a mirror image of the darkest part of yourself.

For you, Warrior, that's exactly what lies ahead. I'm going to be asking you to go head-to-head with what may be the darkest parts of yourself. Complete this next phase of your training, and you will become more powerful than you thought possible. You'll redefine your understanding of what it means to be a warrior.

That, after all, is what I had to do in South Africa. I took Sandra's advice, mustered up a ton of courage, and booked an appointment with a therapist. Her name was Morgan Mitchell, and she had this weird way of not letting me be anything but *real*. It was hard at first, because I was better at hiding behind the mask that I'd created than I was at being my true self.

She started helping me to reset the "broken bones." There were lots of them, more than I imagined. I always thought therapy was, like, lie-on-a-couch-and-talk-about-your-parents-for-an-hour kinda stuff. But the tools and strategies she brought to the table—the

warrior weapons and armor she equipped me with—they started working, man. I learned that the hyenas coming down on me from all sides was legit post-traumatic stress disorder, PTSD. Not just from Mohammed's death, but from the trauma of all sixteen deaths I'd been up close and personal with. Mountaineering accidents. Car accidents. Suicides. Diseases. I was so focused on being tough that I never processed the grief from those. I clung to the toxic *Suck it up* message. Turns out, "suck it up" is a man-mantra that's as weak as a shield made of papier-mâché.

Now, you might be sitting there wondering, *Ummm . . . okay, that got kinda intense all of a sudden. TMI, dude. Isn't it kind of embarrassing to admit those things?*

If you think this is embarrassing (and I would have, too, once), then that's my whole point:

Inner pain is not shameful.

Morgan explained there's nothing disordered about being shaken by trauma, and nothing unnatural about experiencing the response that is built into all humans when we come face to face with a threat. It's called the "fight, flight, freeze, or faint" survival mechanism. All mammals have it. For example, a pit bull will fight. Deer will run or freeze in headlights. A possum will faint. Humans have all of these responses. They're super helpful for surviving saber-toothed tiger attacks, but not so helpful when you're just trying to chill in a café in a foreign country.

Morgan cracked me up when she said it's more likely that someone would be disordered if they were *not* traumatized by something like what happened to me on Everest. PTSD should not have the D, she reasoned. It's just plain "post-traumatic stress."

I imagine you've been through some messed-up stuff in your life, too. I was shown the way out by a great therapist.[1] And by many others—and now I'm turning around and offering to show you the way out. I'm going to equip you with some insanely cool Warrior armor. It's not easy, testing it out as you get bashed into and whatnot. But it'll be so worth it.

As we get you suited up, remember this: Asking for help is not a weakness. No way, man. Asking for help is a *massive* strength.

There you go. Now you know why I'm your Warrior Guide.

---

1   Head to the back of the book in the Resources section for specific info on finding a therapist to talk to.

# TRAINING PHASE II

## DEFENSIVE UPGRADES

I challenge you to see if you can use the same qualities that you feel make you a man to go deeper into yourself. Your strength, your bravery, your toughness. Can we redefine what those mean and use them to explore our hearts? Are you brave enough to be vulnerable? To reach out to another man when you need help? To dive headfirst into your shame? Are you strong enough to be sensitive, to cry whether you are hurting or you're happy, even if it makes you look weak?

—JUSTIN BALDONI, ACTOR AND FEMINIST

# CHALLENGE 4:
# REINFORCE YOUR ARMOR

The difference between successful people and really successful people is really successful people say no to almost everything.

—WARREN BUFFETT,
ONE OF THE GREATEST FINANCIAL
INVESTORS OF ALL TIME

"No" is a complete sentence.

—ANNE LAMOTT,
NOVELIST AND NONFICTION WRITER

# UNRELENTING STANDARDS

The rancid stench of dead fish mixed with wet dog and pine needles floods your nostrils. Fighting your gag reflex, you drag your fingernails through the fatty gel inside the glass jar in front of you, scooping up handful after handful of blubber. You have to be thorough, so you rub the oily globs down your arms and up your thighs, feet, neck, and the hard-to-reach parts of your back. It slowly cakes and dries. You keep dry heaving. And smearing.

It's March and the mountain snow here in your home country of Romania has just begun to melt. Frigid air lashes at your naked skin like an icy whip. You shiver as you press another cold glob against your pale bare chest and smear it everywhere. You hold your breath for as long as possible so you don't have to inhale the reek, but eventually you are forced to take another desperate gasp of air.

*That old fisherman better have been right about this.*

Three months back, you overheard him tell a customer at the open-air market that seal blubber could be used to stay warm while swimming. Your ears perked up and your imagination fired. *That might just work. . . .* As casually as possible, you purchased one of the fisherman's bottles of boiled and rehardened seal blubber. You slipped it into your bag, then smiled and waved at other shop owners to avoid suspicion. Eyes and ears are everywhere here in communist Eastern Europe.

Now, months later, you're covered in blubber and standing almost naked on the riverbank. Fortunately, tonight is the blackest kind of night. No moon and a lot of cloud cover. Perfect for remaining unseen. It's 1974, and your plan is to escape oppressive Romania by swimming across the icy waters of the Danube River, which serves as the border between Romania and Yugoslavia. The Danube is so wide that you can't even see the other side at night. *Crossing these waters will mean freedom. Freedom from oppression, from control, from being told where I can go, who I can talk to, what life I live.*

Spies, security patrols, and armed guards are everywhere: hidden in the trees, tucked away in deserted buildings, driving along the paved and dirt roads alike. They even patrol the river at night by boat and spotlight. This is how your government keeps control of its citizens. This is how they stop you from escaping. You are not a human to these people. To them, you are a resource. No different from metals, timber, oil.

Your whole life, you've been given food rations according to government regulations. You couldn't read books or news that didn't have government approval. While you're guaranteed a job and a roof over your head, that's not what's important to you; your dream is to travel the world. That's impossible, because leaving the country, even for vacation, is illegal. It's also illegal to befriend visitors from other countries. You do it anyway. The government wants to tell you how to think, but your foreign friends have told you stories about what it's like to live as a free citizen. And tonight you're finally demanding freedom for yourself.

For months you've memorized the daily patterns of the military's guards. The river temperatures have warmed from literal ice . . . to icy, and tonight your plan of escape is to look like floating garbage in the Danube. That's why your few belongings are wrapped in a trash bag that you'll also use for flotation in the river current. *They want to treat me like garbage? I'll use garbage to escape.*

If you're caught, it will be clear you were trying to flee. Silence is critical. One cracked twig underfoot could mean years in prison. You need to swim slowly. If they hear splashing, they'll shine lights on you and you'll be shot dead in the water.

The gooey seal fat has now dried and hardened. It feels tight around you, just like a neoprene wetsuit. But *way* more hard-core. *This stuff had better work!* Taking slow, silent steps into the icy river, you wade in up to your knees. You go deeper as the water rises to your thighs. Then your groin (you seriously hesitate). Then your waist. Your belly. Chest . . . And neck.

Your feet lose traction on the rocky river floor, and you begin kicking as slowly as you can, kept afloat by your buoyant trash bag of belongings.

*Don't. Make. Noise.*

Turns out the seal blubber is working! You feel strangely dry. *Only a mile . . . maybe a mile and a half . . . to swim, depending how fast the current is flowing tonight.*

Behind you is the country where your family still lives, not to mention your ex-girlfriend, who wouldn't go with you, and every friend and enemy you've ever had. You love them all, but: *I can't put up with that no more! No way, that ain't for me. Forget. That!*

You kick your way into the blackness and into the gentle waves of small rapids, your hair getting soaked. Your body turns numb from the cold. Still, you kick. Slowly, silently.

Without warning, the top of your foot knocks against a stone. *It's the shore! Of Yugoslavia!*

But despite your ear-to-ear grin and fist pumps at the sky, you have to remain silent. You're not free yet. You could still be shot if a river patrol spots you. You rush to the forest's line of trees, sharp rocks stabbing your frozen feet and lighting them up with pain.

With a smile of elation, you empty your shoes and jeans from the trash bag and put them on. *Still dry! Much better for the walk.* A friend told you that, by foot, it would be two hours west of here until you reach a highway. That's where you're headed. You have no map. No means of finding your way. You've never been in this forest and you're in a communist country with no documentation.

You move swiftly. The motion warms your body, making the numbness subside. You are in the zone. Your eyes see darkness while your mind sees bright visions for your possible future. *No idea what comes next! But I'm not gonna take that treatment anymore, not from anybody. I'm not stopping till I get what I deserve.*

Your anticipation shrinks the hours of bushwhacking into minutes. Soon the highway appears. Thoughts of hitchhiking snap you into self-consciousness and make you wonder what you look like. Worse, what you smell like. Using some dried leaves, you scrape the remaining gelled blobs of seal blubber off your sweaty body.

Your hitchhiking thumb is out and headlights are roaring past you. In minutes, a car comes to a stop. If the driver is a Yugoslavian government official, you'll surely be sent to prison. If it's a citizen, you might hit the jackpot and catch a ride toward the Austrian border. That's where you would like to set up a home temporarily and start applying for citizenship in countries that offer you what you want: true freedom.

The driver of the stopped car leans across the empty passenger seat and cranks down the window by hand.

"Where you going?" he says in Serbo-Croatian-Slovenian. You smile, knowing immediately that he's a friend.

"The Austrian border," you say in his language, trying your best to match his accent.

"I'll take you. Hurry, get in."

You burst with gratitude but try to keep your cool. Highway

miles pass by, and the two of you don't speak. The less you know about each other, the safer you'll both be. You struggle not to nod off. You can't sleep, just in case your driver isn't to be trusted after all.

He slows to a stop along the highway and points the way. He's dropping you a few miles from the Austrian border. For his own safety, he needs to be nowhere close if you end up caught. You shake his hand. You'll never know his name. But he's your hero today. And you know he'll stay your hero for the rest of your life.

You make your way to the Austrian border. *You can see it!* In your excitement, you begin running. *This is it! Freedom!*

You step on a branch.

It cracks.

Two guards snap their flashlights in your direction. You had no

idea they were there. They have dogs and AK-47s. *Kalashnikovs,* they call them in Russian. The silence turns into chaos. They're screaming, ordering you to the ground. You're no match for their weapons and you can't outrun the canines, so you do as they say. A steel-toed boot catches you hard in your rib cage. Then another in your stomach. You roll onto your back, and the blunt end of an AK-47 bashes you in the forehead. You're knocked out.

You wake with your hands cuffed to one of the guards. The other is several meters behind you with his gun trained on you.

You're forced to your feet, and the guy with the gun barrel pointed at your back tells you it's time to march.

For several hours, they tell you nothing. Finally, you arrive at an armored tank. You're shoved inside and cuffed to the piping. The tank rolls you to a prison, to a future that promises to be anything but bright.

# WALLY STIRBU: BOUNDARIES ARE YOUR ARMOR

After he was captured, True Warrior Viorel "Wally" Stirbu spent three months in a communist Yugoslavian prison. Behind bars, he met a local who taught him the security pattern of the Yugoslavia-Austria border guards. *Now that I know what went wrong, I can improve my next attempt,* Wally thought.

He was then transferred to a Romanian jail, where he spent another year in captivity.

After being released, he was informed that a second escape attempt would result in three years in prison. Even so, Wally knew his ultimate goal was to live as a citizen of a free country. Nothing less was acceptable.

That's why, even with the threat of jail time, Wally spent the next year and a half planning and scouting his exact route for a second escape attempt. Wally again bought seal blubber from the grizzled fisherman, crossed the icy Danube by cover of night, and hitchhiked across Yugoslavia. Then, using his new knowledge of the security-guard pattern, he sat, cloaked in the darkness of the forest, and waited. When the coast was finally clear, he made his move and crossed the border! His legs were like Jell-O from excitement and disbelief. He was walking on Austrian soil. He'd made it! His life could be . . . anything he wanted it to be.

While working odd jobs for cash, Wally began writing to other countries' governments and asking if they would let him become a citizen. Austria had a ten-year waiting period for becoming a citizen, but he couldn't wait that long, so he decided to move to the first country that would take him. He applied to Australia, Germany, England, Canada, everywhere that would give him an application.

From the age of twenty-four until he was twenty-nine, Wally refused to lower his standards. "As long as they have freedom of speech and they gonna let me travel? I didn't care," Wally told me. "But you know who took me? The greatest country in the entire world. That was the United States."

Wally and I met on a climbing expedition in Indonesia, where he shared his story with me. He also shared that he became a Chicago city firefighter. And that he's climbed the tallest mountain on every continent except for Asia. (He's got two attempts on Everest and, last I spoke to Wally, he's going for a third!)

Wally's True Warrior trait is being able to say no to what he doesn't deserve and yes to what he does. Crossing the boundary that is the Danube was the moment he made clear to himself and to everyone around him what he was—and was not—going to put up with. He looked at his situation and said, *I don't like this. I deserve better than this. I'm not putting up with it. I'm doing whatever it takes to be treated like the independent man of integrity that I am.*

True Warriors say the same.

# WHAT BOUNDARIES DO FOR YOU

What do you do when someone comes along and threatens the values in your Warrior Creed? How do you defend yourself? How do you stop another person—or a group of people—from negatively impacting you and compromising the person you aim to become?

Maybe a better, simpler way to ask that is: How do you stop other people from making you feel like crap sometimes?

Answer: You set boundaries for yourself.

Boundaries are a True Warrior's heavy armor. They're your plate mail, your chain mail, your shield, greaves, and gauntlets, all in one skill. Your boundaries are how you defend your values and how you protect your crew, your tribe, and yourself. They're how you stick up for your inherent rights as a human being.

Just as chain mail stops you from taking hits, stabs, hacks, and arrows that would otherwise slice through your body, your boundaries define what you will and will not stand for. You get to decide what treatment you will accept from other people. And you get to express what you expect from them, as long as you communicate it in a healthy way.

**Challenge 4 is to establish boundaries of your own that will protect you and your tribe. To succeed at this, you'll need to respectfully state—and enforce—what is okay and not okay with you. You'll need to set boundaries not only with others, but also with yourself.**

Of all the challenges in this book, this is the most important for you to master and carry with you throughout your life.

Boundaries are how men can be compassionate, fierce, firm, and respectful all at once. Instead of acting like a tough jerk, being a people-pleasing nice guy, or numbing yourself, boundaries help you get what's good and healthy for yourself and for the people in your tribe.

By the end of this challenge, you will know the answers to these questions:

- What behaviors and treatment will I not accept?
- What standards do I hold myself to?
- What standards do I expect from the people around me?
- What are my body's boundaries?
- How do I stop myself from being manipulated?
- How do I tell somebody no and still stay friends with them?

Perhaps more important than anything, boundaries are how you defend your Warrior Creed. That's critical, because whatever comes from the truest part of you is *absolutely* worth defending.

# WHY WARRIORS NEED DEFENSES

I can hear you over there, getting all squirmy and weird as you read this. "But, John, I don't want to exclude anybody! I want to break down walls, not build them up!"

I hear you, and you're a good person for wanting to build bridges, not obstacles. Bravo, my man.

But we aren't talking about stonewalling or ignoring people. Even though it seems counterintuitive, boundaries actually help us to *improve* our relationships.

Dr. Henry Cloud and Dr. John Townsend wrote a whole series of books about this one subject. These guys are like the mob bosses of boundary setting, the ones everybody looks to on this subject.

They say that "a boundary is a property line that defines where you end, and someone else begins." For the things that are legitimately yours, boundaries say, "This is my property, and on my property, we respect the rules of my house."

Make sense?

Let's roll with that idea, that a Warrior's armor is a "property line."

Pretend for a moment that every day when you get home from school, you wave hi to your neighbor Bob, unlock the door, then walk inside. You're home! You plug in your phone, make a sandwich, and then plop down on your bed for a nap. You love every second of this part of your day.

Now imagine that, one day, you get home and Bob's not outside. Oddly, your front door is wide open. You nervously wander in, on guard in your own home. *This is weird,* you think. *And kind of scary.*

You go to plug in your phone and there's a bright orange extension cord plugged into the outlet you normally use. You follow the extension cord straight into your room, and *voilà!* There's Bob, your next-door neighbor. He's jumping on your bed with muddy boots! When he turns to say hi, bread crumbs and chunks of peanut butter spray out of his mouth and across your room. He's eaten all your food! Through gobs of peanut butter, he says, "Okay, Google! Play some music!" and he suddenly starts rocking out to a disco ball that he's drilled into your ceiling and powered up with the orange extension cord.

Question for you . . . what would you say to your neighbor Bob?

The entry-level beginner boundary setter would probably say, "Grrrraaaargh! Get out! I'm calling the cops!" And that would be perfectly within your rights.

But remember how, a few pages ago, you were complaining that you don't want to exclude people or build up walls? If you applied that here, you'd do what many people do when they need to have uncomfortable interactions with people: say nothing and try to let it go. After all, you don't want to make Bob feel bad about himself or unwelcome. Plus your parents might be upset if you were rude to the neighbor. So instead, you try to nap on the kitchen floor, all sorts of resentful. You're hungry and tired, and your phone is dead.

Disco-ball-rocking, bed-jumping Bob finally leaves. You figure it'll just be a one-time event, so you clean up his mess.

But the next thing you know, Bob is coming over every single day, doing the same thing. Only now . . . he's bringing his friends to party!

You're trying to be cool with it, you really are. But one day, you snap. You unload on the dude. All sorts of verbal venom comes pouring out of your face. You're fuming! You let him have it as you dump every ounce of your built-up anger and frustration on the guy, your rebuke full of curse words. The music stops and everyone blinks in shock at your tirade.

*End scene.*

Let me ask you: Who's the jerk in this scenario?

Hint . . . it's not Bob.

It's you.

*Wait, whaaaa?!*

Yeah, you acted aggressively. While you may be justified in feeling frustrated and angry at Bob and the whole neighborhood, it's *you* who attacked *him*. You took out your anger on Bob in a verbally violent way.

It's your responsibility to tell people when they are doing things that make you uncomfortable. It's your responsibility to enforce the consequences that you've been clear about. That's why it's *you* who's the jerk for snapping and yelling at him. Bob had absolutely no idea he'd been upsetting you. He thought you loved it when he came over. After all, you never told him anything different. You never set a boundary.

While this may be an exaggerated story, the point is that, for everything in your life that's your "property"—and that goes for your life plans, your thoughts, your emotions, your body, your stuff, your secrets, your time—you get to choose what's okay and what's not okay. And then it's your responsibility to communicate those rules to other people.

Let me put this in giant bold letters so there's no question about what I'm saying:

**It is your human right to decide what you will and will not accept as treatment from any person or group of people. You should say no to any treatment that makes you uncomfortable. You have every right to ask—and require—that your standards be met.**

# A WARRIOR'S RIGHTS

We say that our human rights are life, liberty, and the pursuit of happiness. Well, shoot me off a firework and sing "Yankee Doodle Dandy," what in the world does that mean?

Everyone has human rights, just by being alive. Wally decided that it was his human right to live in a country that would allow him to travel wherever he pleased and be friends with whoever he wanted. In the same way, you are allowed to defend what you believe your rights to be, as long as you're not hurting someone else.

Respecting yourself and believing that boundaries are in fact *your human right* is the critical first step in setting boundaries. Because, really, if your opinion of yourself sucks, how can you possibly expect anyone else to give you high-quality treatment? If you want others to respect you, you've first gotta respect yourself.

## DON'T STAB YOURSELF

You start by making sure that your armor protects you from you.

Yeah, you read that sentence correctly.

You've got to start by having rules in place for what you won't tolerate from yourself!

*Hang on, I thought this was about defending myself from other people!*

Yeah, it's that, too.

But you start with wearing armor that stops you from accidentally stabbing yourself.

Do you know the things that you, with certainty, won't let yourself do? Can you state with 100 percent confidence the standards that you require from yourself? In other words, your boundaries with yourself.

Here are some examples I've heard from other people. You don't have to take on all of them . . . but you could!

## PEOPLE GET TO HAVE BOUNDARIES ABOUT THEIR PHYSICAL HEALTH.

- I don't eat meat.
- I need eight hours of sleep, so no matter what, I get ready for bed at ten p.m.
- I take a vitamin every morning.

## PEOPLE GET TO HAVE BOUNDARIES ABOUT THEIR MINDS.

- I complete my homework after school, before answering texts or messages.
- I journal one page per day.
- I don't bring any screens into my bedroom, including my phone.

## PEOPLE GET TO HAVE BOUNDARIES ABOUT THEIR GOALS.

- I practice hockey drills for an hour a day, no matter what.
- I read my faith's religious text each evening.
- I meditate with an app every morning.
- I spend every Monday evening with my family.

## PEOPLE GET TO HAVE BOUNDARIES ABOUT THEIR STUFF.

- I don't sit in front of other students who kick my chair in class.
- I make my bed every morning as a sign of self-respect.
- I don't share my phone or email password with friends or the person I'm dating.

## PEOPLE GET TO HAVE BOUNDARIES ABOUT HOW THEY INTERACT WITH OTHERS.

- I won't tolerate abuse of any kind, not from anyone or toward anyone.
- I smile and chat with randoms because it's fun to improve people's days.
- I don't have any social media at all because I want to interact with the real world.
- I don't ever send inappropriate photos of myself to anyone at all.

## PEOPLE GET TO HAVE BOUNDARIES ABOUT ELECTRONICS.

- I don't bring my phone to a table where I'm sharing a meal.
- I video chat with my cousin/friend/grandpa/nephew each Sunday.
- I have a screen-time limit and stick to it.

Now it's your turn. What are the things that you absolutely will not compromise on? You can seriously choose anything you like!

Here's the key: If you set that boundary, then it's something that you either DO—or you DON'T. Plain and simple. It's a matter of fact.

If it's something you DO, then your tone of voice should be the same as if you were saying, "I guarantee you I brush my teeth, at a bare minimum, once every week." It's like, *Umm, yeah, of course! Anything less would be super weird and uncomfortable!*

And if it's something you don't do? Then it's like you're saying, "I don't chew bark on trees." Like, *Duh! I have zero percent desire for that. No way.*

Sometimes it's hard to get to there, to believe you deserve your boundaries. But you do. So aim to say 'em in that tone.

At any point, on any day, you can make a boundary for yourself. If you suddenly remember that you don't like yogurt, you can say, "I don't eat yogurt. Not my thing." Boom. Personal boundary set.

If you ever go to a party where people are drinking alcohol and you realize it isn't a fun experience, you can say, "I don't go to parties where there's alcohol." You can also say, "I don't drink alcohol." Those would be slam dunks on great personal boundaries.

After setting boundaries with yourself, you're ready to set them with other people. There are levels of difficulty here. In fact, it's precisely like the *Halo* video game series! Your boundaries can be Normal . . . Heroic. Or . . . LEGENDARY!

Here's what's cool when it comes to setting boundaries with other people: as long as your boundaries don't hurt anyone else or yourself, then you can set a boundary for anything you want! Boundaries are meant to protect your rights, like your right to privacy. They're *not* used to punish somebody, make their life worse, or control them.

With that said, you ready to throw down, Warrior?

# NORMAL BOUNDARY SETTING

The first time you try setting a boundary, like you did with Bob, you might just be like, "Get out of here!" And that works as a boundary because all you have to do is ask yourself, "What do I want?" and then tell 'em what you came up with.

Normal mode boundary setting is just saying precisely what you don't want. "Stop!" and "No!" and "I'm leaving!" and "You shall not pass!" are also examples. Not the worst. Also not . . . the best approach. Because nobody likes being told what to do.

But how do you figure out what you want?

**1.** Ask yourself: Does this make me feel good, in a healthy way?

**2.** Ask yourself: Does this NOT make me feel good, in an unhealthy way?

That's usually all you need. If you STILL can't figure out what you want? Here's an awesome life hack: Pretend it's not even about you. Follow author Dr. Robert Glover's advice and ask, how would a healthy man handle this situation? That question, he says, will massively help guys connect with their inner wisdom and figure out what's right for them.

# HEROIC BOUNDARY SETTING

Three parts to this one. You're on it!

### PART 1: DESCRIBE WHAT YOU SEE HAPPENING.

The only thing you're doing in the first part is describing what you're seeing. You're not judging, criticizing, or complaining. You're not getting in their face. You're just stating facts.

Example: "I see you are coming over to my house every day and using my stuff, and you didn't ask me if you could."

### PART 2: SAY YOU DON'T LIKE IT.

Example: "I don't like it."

### PART 3: GIVE 'EM A CHANCE TO MAKE IT RIGHT.

Here, you just tell someone how they can make it right in your eyes. You're not "getting back" at them. You're just pretending they asked you the question, "What can I do to fix it?"—even if they didn't, assume they wanna stay cool with you and tell 'em how they can do that.

Example: "In the future, please promise you'll ask if you wanna come over again."

# LEGENDARY BOUNDARY SETTING

This is it! The granddaddy of all boundary-setting methods! Play at this level and doves will land on your outstretched arms and unicorns will bow at your feet.

All you're going to do is add in two components on top of Heroic mode.

First, add: *Name your negative feeling.*

You know how we have three primary colors? Well, we also only have three primary negative feelings. They are:

Sad—Mad—Scared

Everything else is a blend of those three. So when you set a Legendary boundary, you only have to worry about picking the one of the three that's closest to what you're feeling. You aren't trying to convince the other person of anything.

With Bob, Legendary would look like: "Hey, dude, you broke into my house and that's why I'm feeling really mad right now."

You're basically saying, "Hey, I'm human, I'm hurting over this thing you're doing. You're human, too. Can we reconnect?"

# WARNING! WARNING! DANGER AHEAD!

**Pay close attention: Don't confuse "feelings" with "being judgmental."**

If you were to say to someone, "I feel you're being a jerk right now," that is not describing what you're feeling. That's you being judgmental.

"Jerk" isn't a feeling. It's a name. If you say "I feel like you're being a jerk," you are actually just disguising your name-calling behind the label of "my feelings."

If you think someone is acting like a jerk, that's a belief. It's not a feeling.

> "I feel that you"—followed by anything else—should not be said when naming your feelings because that's just pointing a finger.

The second new component in Legendary mode boundary setting is to explain what will happen if the other person doesn't make it right. It's stating the consequences for them: "Bob, if you aren't out in ten minutes and my place isn't cleaned, I'm going to call the police to have them arrest you for trespassing."

You're calmly saying, "Yes, you can choose to do this thing that makes me uncomfortable. And if you decide to, then I will make my decision about how to respond. Now you know in advance what that response will be."

## LEGENDARY BOUNDARY SETTING PROCESS

**PART 1**: Say what you're seeing.

**PART 2**: Name what it makes you feel.

**PART 3**: Give 'em a chance to make it right.

**PART 4**: Explain the consequence if they don't make it right.

## OTHER PEOPLE GET BOUNDARIES, TOO

If you expect your boundaries to be respected, you've got to respect other people's boundaries. Yeah, didn't think of that one, did you?

Other people get to say no. They get to enforce healthy consequences. People are even allowed to not respect your boundaries (and you are then allowed to enforce healthy consequences).

Like, if you decide you're not going to do your homework assignment and call it your right to set a boundary, then you'll have to expect your teacher's boundary of giving you an F.

Your parents also get to set boundaries with you as long as they're respecting your human rights. If you're going to live in their house or houses, they get to ask you to live by their house rules. If they want the lights off when you leave, want your bed made, or want you home at a certain time, respect their boundaries. And remember, parents are people. They may not be Legendary boundary setters yet, so be patient and kind with them.

# LIVING FREE

Last I spoke with Wally, he had just run the Chicago marathon and was preparing to take a tropical vacation with his girlfriend. Without epic boundary setting, the life he's lived would not have been possible. That's because setting boundaries is the only path to real freedom.

In your case, I can't wait for you to tell me someday that you can say no without guilt, that you can ask for what you need, that you can disagree with someone and still feel safe, that you can tell someone that they've upset you without it turning into a big deal, and that you can say "Yes" to the things you really want with your whole heart. Those are the hallmark traits of a Warrior who has staked his claim on his own freedom!

# TRAINING GROUNDS:
## REINFORCE YOUR ARMOR

### KNOW IT

Boys throw tantrums or shut down when their rights are violated. True Warriors set boundaries to guard their Warrior Creed and to connect with people. Boundaries ensure the protection of freedoms, friendships, and romances!

### ACT ON IT

☐ Review the examples of boundaries you could set for yourself on pages 108–109. Are any of those important to you? Take 'em on as your own!

☐ What treatment do you accept and expect from yourself? Create three new boundaries of your own. Commit to follow these rules that define you!

☐ The next time you notice that you're in a tense situation, set a boundary with the person or people involved. Return to the defense manual beginning on page 111 and see whether you set your boundary in Normal, Heroic, or Legendary mode.

# CHALLENGE 5: FORM YOUR BATTLE CREW

I'm not one of those people who expresses or articulates feelings very well, but from now on, just know this: It's on, man. It is *on*. You know what I'm saying? We're in a fight, and you can count on me until the last man is standing. Somewhere up there is a star with your name on it. I might not be able to help you find it, but I've got pretty strong shoulders, and you can stand on my shoulders while you're looking for that star. You hear? For as long as you want. Stand on my shoulders and reach, man. Reach.

—GIL REYES, TRAINER AND FRIEND TO ANDRE AGASSI, ONE OF THE GREATEST TENNIS PLAYERS OF ALL TIME, FROM AGASSI'S AUTOBIOGRAPHY, *OPEN*

# THE DAWN WALL

You pull with bone-crushing force against the razor edges of rock in front of you. The only thing stopping you from plunging toward the rocky, tree-covered valley floor is the strength of your grip on these sharpened, dime-sized granite edges. You're as high as a 140-story building and dangling by millimeters of skin contact. Sure, you're attached to an 8.5-millimeter-thick rope, but a fall will still send you free-falling for a potentially backbreaking forty feet before you're yanked to a stop by the double-figure-eight knot tied to your harness.

Your movement is precise and powerful, evidence of a life spent bouldering. Climbing ten- to twenty-foot-tall, super-hard routes has been your thing since you were a teenager. Pebble Wrestler was your nickname, and you are still one of the world's elite. So skilled, in fact, that you were once featured in a movie about your "send" up an unthinkable forty-five-foot bouldering route in California named Ambrosia. At that height, and without a rope, you were pushing the limits of the sport and blurring the lines between bouldering and free-solo climbing.

That was six years ago.

Now, "send" is still climber slang for completing a route without falling, but Ambrosia has become a distant memory. That was child's play compared to the rock you're on right now. This is so next-level that the cold, gray-brown granite in front of you has bright red stains of your blood smeared across it. You're not even halfway up this half-mile-high wall, and so far, it's acting like an endless cheese grater for human flesh. You haven't slept in a bed—let alone walked on solid earth—in eleven days.

You're dangling by your fingertips on the side of El Capitan. It's an epic, 3,000-foot-tall, massive block of stone in Yosemite National Park. Multiple nearby waterfalls, each hundreds of feet tall, are dwarfed by the granite tower you're climbing. This particular vertical route up El Cap is called the Dawn Wall. By the standards of the world's most elite climbers, this is considered the hardest climb in existence. In fact, no one has ever successfully climbed it. And you, more than anyone, know why: You've been trying for *six years*. On this attempt alone, you've been hanging on this wall for nearly *two weeks* now. Little by little, you and your climbing partner, Tommy, have been trying to figure out how to successfully link together each puzzle piece of the climb. For months on end, you've come out here together in the blistering heat/freezing cold/rain/snow/doesn't-matter-let's-go-climbing weather. The elements have made your otherwise fair skin lightly sunburned and the lack of bathroom conveniences means your goatee is growing out.

The goal for you and Tommy is to get to the top of El Cap's Dawn Wall in a single attempt—the whole thing, section by section, without falling. Each section of a climb is called a pitch, and you're on the fifteenth pitch out of thirty-two. You've taken turns, one belaying the other while he flails to figure out each incremental move.

The fifteenth is the "crux" pitch. It's the hardest of the whole 3,000-foot climb. This is where it always falls apart . . . for you, for Tommy, and for . . . well, that's it, actually. You're the only two climbers who have ever climbed this high on the Dawn Wall. Here, the rock resembles a polished bowling ball. There's not even a dimple big enough to catch a fingernail on.

Since this adventure began, Tommy has been the visionary. He is one of the most skilled and versatile rock climbers in human history. Six years ago, the two of you were featured in a climbing documentary called *Progression*. Tommy's segment shows his first attempts on the Dawn Wall. He'd be dangling by a rope *for days at a time,* just staring at small sections of the rock for hours on end, not talking to anyone, and barely eating or sleeping. Yet he was never able to climb it.

At the end of the doc, Tommy said, "Even if I can't climb it, I want to plant the seed for someone in the future to come and inspire us all." It felt like he was throwing down the gauntlet. Like his giant head was projected on the big screen and suddenly looked at you, saying, "You think you've got what it takes?"

Gauntlet thrown.

You tracked down his email address and asked Tommy Caldwell, one of the greatest climbers of all time, if he needed a belay partner. It was the climbing equivalent of you asking Michael Jordan if he needs some help with his free throws.

To your utter shock, Tommy got back to you and said, "Yes!"

He took you under his wing and showed you how to be comfortable up here, in the snow, in the heat, in the dark. He had eighteen years of experience climbing El Cap. You had zero years of experience on big walls. You didn't know how to manage ropes, you couldn't carry days' worth of water, you couldn't haul bags of equipment and food—let alone rig a tent for safe cliffside sleeping. You started as an apprentice.

That feels like it was ages ago. Now you refocus on the rock face and reach your hand into the chalk bag dangling around your waist. The magnesium carbonate powder is meant to dry out the biohazard of blood, sweat, and dirt that's soaked through your bandages. A snowlike cloud of chalk particles whips out of your bag and dances through the icy wind. The airborne dust draws your attention to your tent. The thing is literally hanging from the side of the cliff, suspended in the air. It's called a portaledge because first, *porta* (portable) and second, *ledge* (a ledge to sleep on). The surface is barely bigger than a twin bed and it's a quarter of an inch thick. Covered only by a nylon sheet, this is where you and Tommy sleep, eat, text, and tweet. Home, sweet home.

The official rules for any legitimate climber? Once on the wall, you can't touch the ground. You can try each pitch as many times as you want, spending as long as you want to recover. But eventually, to "succeed," you have to climb each pitch, in order, without falling, and without touching the valley floor. That's why you've been up here for eleven days now.

You take a breath as you ready yourself for the crux move. The only conceivable way past the crux pitch is to leap. Yes, while 1,450 feet above the ground, you have to jump eight feet and grab on to a knife-edge rail. You've attempted it thousands of times and failed each time. You don't know how or why this attempt will be any different, but with each attempt, it feels a hairline fracture closer to being possible. To get it done, you need something other than strength. You need skin. You need contact and grip. But your medical tape is oozing blood again, and your hand is slipping. Before you can regain your hold, you're falling backward. You grip harder. But the skin of your right index finger ruptures, busting open and sending more blood everywhere.

You curse and scream in pain and frustration before yelling out to Tommy, "Falling!"

Your rope jerks you to a halt, and you again dangle beneath the portaledge. You didn't get anywhere.

Tommy is silent. You climb up the rope back to him and your hanging shelter. You're exhausted, frustrated, and overwhelmed. Your self-confidence is even more shredded than your fingertips.

After you guys debrief, Tommy suggests you spend two full days resting your fingers. You agree. While you'd ideally climb pitch for pitch with him, you decide together that he'll climb ahead while your hands heal.

Harder than climbing is waiting. As you sit 1,450 feet in the sky, you promptly get sucked into your phone. Whether or not you can scale this thing has made its way into the collective consciousness of the entire country. Even the *New York Times* is writing daily updates about your status. Until now, you've checked in only periodically, but word is out that you're struggling, and your phone's blowing up with texts, calls, and DMs from every person you've ever met. You're even trending on Twitter. Every major news outlet has written about you. News vans arrive in the valley, and they've trained their telephoto lenses right on your tent. The world is watching. *As if going to the bathroom up here wasn't hard enough!*

The spotlight and attention only amplify the voice of your wicked little inner roommate: *You're not enough. And you started this whole mess! You tweeted live updates and brought all this attention to yourself. Now everyone is going to see that you can't do this.*

Tommy picks up on your anxiety. "They're way down there. We're way up here. Relax. Be here, not there."

Then your mentor and climbing partner does something incredible.

"Oh, crap! I just dropped my phone," he says matter-of-factly.

Your eyes bug out of your head as you clench your own phone tighter in your hand. "Seriously? No way . . . you're joking."

He puts both arms in the air, shrugging. He swears that it was an accident, that it slipped from his pocket. But here's a guy who's literally been climbing since he could walk. He's summited more big-wall projects than perhaps anyone who has ever lived. The guy doesn't accidentally drop things.

But there went his iPhone, cascading down the cliff, splintering into a billion little pieces. "You know what, dude, I'm psyched," he says. "This is going to allow me to fully embrace the rest of this experience. I'm going to keep going until Wino Tower but stop there. I'll go into full support mode at that point for as long as it takes for you to catch up. There's nothing worse I could imagine than finishing this climb without you."

*This guy has caught my falls a thousand times. He's mentored me for six years. On this push, he's waited for me on this pitch for a week. He could've continued on without me. Now he's chucked his phone off a cliff and is jeopardizing his own shot at success just because he wants to do it together with me. This dude has my back.*

You give Tommy your full support to continue climbing higher.

He's slaying pitch after pitch, getting higher as you rest. In the evening, he rappels down to your shared portaledge. Then, in the morning, he shimmies back up the rope network to continue climbing from where he left off. As long as he doesn't touch the valley floor, he can go up and down the cliff as many times as he wants to work each pitch. He's *crushing*. This is the most impressive, focused, in-the-zone climbing you've ever seen in your life. It's next-level.

On the second night of your two nights of rest, Tommy's confidence bleeds into yours. You stir your tea and say, "I know I can do that pitch."

"Yeah, for sure you can," Tommy says instantly.

Tommy doesn't make a big speech because, to Tommy, there's nothing he's trying to convince you of. For him, believing in your ability to climb this thing is a given.

Day fourteen arrives. Your time to rest is done. Your fingers are as good as they'll get. It's time to *send* or go home.

It's go time. It's January, which means the cold temperatures make the rubber on your shoes stick to the wall just a tiny bit better. Every microscopic advantage you can get, you take. You sandpaper the soles of your climbing shoes to give them a fresh start, then superglue the cuts on your fingers together, weaving an elaborate tape job around them. You check your equipment and tie into your rope. Tommy puts you on belay. You commit to getting the job done. It's not overconfidence. It's not egotistical. It's a calm resolve and acknowledgment of the simple fact: This is going to happen.

You go through the starting moves and fall. You consider it your warm-up.

A few hours pass and you're fully in the zone. This time, you decide to go at it differently. You decide you're going to climb *through* the crux move. No more jump.

You traverse out to the crux move of the crux pitch. You move into position. Your gaze drops to your feet, and you gingerly place your toes on rock dimples that are no wider than the ridged edge of a quarter.

You look back at Tommy. Even though it's silent, you know him so well that you can feel his thoughts. He's cheering you on, practically trying to force your hands and feet to stick by telekinesis. *That dude has my back. That dude makes me better. That dude respects my boundaries.*

You're spread-eagled, splayed across the wall. An icy updraft blows up your shirt and your pant legs. You shift your mind from relaxation to a laser focus. You exhale sharply a few times, preparing for the intensity of what you're about to do.

# KEVIN JORGESON: WHO ARE YOUR PEOPLE?

With mutant-level strength, delicate precision, and demigod levels of self-control, True Warrior Kevin Jorgeson became the first human to ever climb through the Dawn Wall's crux move. By the end of the pitch, gobs of blood were dripping from his hand, spilling out of five massive fissures in his torn-up fingers.

It was such an epic, inspiring feat that soon afterward, Apple made El Cap the default background image on every one of their computers. And it stayed the name of their operating system for three straight years.

There's a rating scale that climbers use for the difficulty of climbs. If you can climb 5.12, you're an advanced climber. Climb 5.13 and you can get sponsored; it's experts only. The Dawn Wall crux pitch is

5.14c. The world's most elite climbers would struggle on this pitch, even if they were coming at it right off the ground with fresh muscles. Most would also be exhausted for days. In a row, Kevin climbed a 5.14d, a 5.14c, a 5.14a corner, and then three more pitches of hard 5.13 until he caught up to Tommy at Wino Tower.

On day nineteen, Tommy and Kevin "topped out" and were hailed as heroes. Even President Barack Obama requested to meet them. They were guests on morning, daytime, and prime-time talk shows on every major news network. In these interviews, never did they brag. Kevin didn't say, "Yeah, I was the only one who did the crux move on pitch fifteen," and Tommy didn't say, "Yeah, but I waited seven days for you to catch up."

Instead, they each knew that neither could have succeeded without the other. Together, they made each other stronger. Tommy had been considering quitting the attempt altogether back before Kevin emailed and brought fresh energy to the project.

Relationships are your life's greatest asset. That's why all guys, like all great climbers, need a rock-solid Battle Crew. In fact, Ryan Michler, host of the *Order of Man* podcast series, says, "The 'lone wolf' idea for men is flawed at best, destructive at its worst." The solution, he says, is for every guy to have a battle team in place. We're talking the kind of team that will make you a better person. The kind that respects your boundaries. And the kind that has your back when you need them. More than any other outside influence, it's the people you decide to spend your time with who will define your life experience.

These people are different from your tribe. Your Battle Crew is the handful of people you allow to get closest to you, your tightest circle. It's the family you choose for yourself. Your crew should definitely include friends, but it could also include your parents, siblings, teachers, coaches, or mentors.

So how do you assemble your Battle Crew? How do you keep the wrong people out? That's what this challenge is all about: you're going to form a crew of your own.

**Challenge 5 is to run the three-part crew member check on every person who's close to you. You will succeed at this challenge by selecting a Battle Crew that's made up of two to five people . . . then continuing to run this check on the new people who come into your life.**

Here's a big ol' no-duh: our friends influence us. Study after study shows that if your friends are successful, you're more likely to be successful. If your friends are unhealthy, there's a good chance you'll make unhealthy choices. If your friends make good grades, you probably will, too.

But get this . . . social scientist David Burkus discovered that the friends of your friends will still affect you, even if you don't know them! He proved a simple, factual point: the people you choose to hang around—and the people they choose to hang around—have a massive, undeniable influence on who you become.

Your relationships define your life experience, so you should surround yourself with people who are freaking amazing.

Is your crew raising you up or dragging you down? Do the people surrounding you inspire you or discourage you? Really think about each person you spend your time with. See their faces. Name them. One at a time, as you think of them, ask yourself three questions about them:

## THE 3-PART BATTLE-CREW QUALIFICATION CHECKLIST

**1. Does this person make me better?**

**2. Does this person have my back?**

**3. Does this person respect my boundaries?**

A friend who has earned their place as your friend—by passing this three-part check—is worth their weight in gold. But if you can't answer yes to all three of those questions? That person doesn't deserve to be a part of your Battle Crew.

# WHO AREN'T YOUR PEOPLE

I am giving you full permission, right now, not to be friends with anyone you don't want to be friends with. In fact, I'm giving you wild encouragement to be ruthless about who you do, and don't, let into your inner circle.

People who don't bring out the best in you, and especially people who treat you poorly, should be excluded from your crew. I'm not saying be a jerk or treat people rudely. Instead, simply leave people out of your life if they don't support your values.

It's not about choosing friends who are perfect or never make mistakes. Part of being a man is being able to work through disagreements with your crew members once in a while and come out better because of it. That's healthy.

But the idea that you need to accept absolutely everyone and that you should be tolerant of all behavior no matter what? That's a bunch of garbage. I'm with writer and poet S. C. Lourie, who says, "You will be too raw for some. You will be too loud, too big, too fierce, too quiet, too deep. These are not your people."

Love people? Yes. Be a great example? Absolutely. But let other people influence you when they haven't earned it? No way.

Of course there will be school projects, teams, jobs, classes, and events where you have to interact with people who don't pass the three-part crew check. That's okay, because nobody is required to make you better, have your back, or respect your boundaries.

# HOW TO CREATE YOUR OWN CREW

If you want friends who pass the check, YOU have to pass it first! Do you make the other person better? Do you have the other person's back? Do you respect the other person's boundaries? Fortunately, after completing Challenges 1 through 4, it's very likely that you do.

Next, you've got to see who else wants in.

To make a blanket statement here, I find that girls are naturally better at this than guys. They can often connect just by talking. In my experience, dudes can't. We need to do something together. I mean, there's no way that Tommy and Kevin would have spent a cumulative year together, just talking. Bonding without a shared task, sport, job, or hobby is hard for us! We gotta do somethin'!

I mean, can you imagine inviting somebody to go hunting if killing an animal wasn't a part of it? "Hey, Steve, you wanna walk ten miles through a swamp so that we can lie down in some really sharp brambles together until we're so cold that we can't feel our feet?"

"Gee, I dunno. We gonna do anything?"

"Nah. Just talk."

Sounds ridiculous, right? But throw in "We're gonna handle lethal weapons," and suddenly you've got camo-wearing, bow-and-arrow-buying buddies who will bond and connect while they hunt together.

And if you don't hunt—I personally don't—then there are plenty of other options. I have rock climbing, mountaineering, kite-surfing, and public speaking. It's through those things that I've met my crew and bonded with some amazingly high-quality people. My closest friends are the buddies I've battled cliff faces and glacier fields with. My crew are the dudes I've been tossed by ten-foot waves with.

What are you so passionate about that you would study, talk about, practice, and buy things related to that thing, no matter what? What do you LOVE to do?

That's where you start. Pick something *you* want to do. You don't have to have a reason. It just has to sound fun.

Then just ask a few dudes who seem cool if they also want to go do that thing with you. Don't make it weird or difficult. Keep it simple. *Dude, you wanna float inner tubes down the river? Dude, you wanna go to the batting cages? Dude, you wanna hit up the roller coasters this weekend? Dude, you wanna learn wilderness survival? Dude, you wanna go to church? Dude, you wanna meditate? Dude, you wanna play football? Dude, you wanna hit the skate* park? *Dude, you wanna take dance lessons? Dude, you wanna climb a mountain? Dude, you wanna go to a leadership conference? Dude, you wanna protest environmental policy? Dude, you wanna go lie down in the brambles and freeze our butts off and shoot at things?*

And if he doesn't want to do your thing, respect his boundaries. Don't make a big deal out of it, and move on to someone else. Nothing lost, nothing gained.

CAUTION: If someone says yes, remember that they're not a part of your crew yet! Whatever you do together is your chance to find out if he actually passes the three-part crew check. Here's what that is:

## Q1: HOW DOES THAT DUDE MAKE ME BETTER?

Plain and simple: You want people in your Battle Crew who will improve your life.

Someone is not your friend just because they make you laugh. They're not your friend because they entertain you. They're not your friend because you have something that they want or because they can use you as a stepping-stone—those are takers.

How can you know when someone makes you better? The easy way is when they're better than you at a specific skill. Their abilities will rub off on you, just like you'll lose pounds when your friends lose weight. Weird but true! That's exactly why I try to surround myself with people I admire who are better than me at . . . well, basically everything! Even cooler, my bros are genuinely excited when I start to catch up!

Just by asking to hang out with people—male or female—whose skills I admire and then learning from them, I've been able to accomplish some world-class feats. That's precisely what I did with climbing. I sought out friends who could help me improve. Next thing you know, I had reached the tops of the world's tallest mountains.

Friendship works best, though, when you're also a mentor in your own way. Real men help each other improve! It's straight outta the Bible. Proverbs 27:17 says, "As iron sharpens iron, so one person sharpens another."

What value do you bring to your friends' lives? Can you help them study for their tests? Can you show them how to throw a ball for maximum accuracy or how to land a kick flip on a skateboard? If your buddy has a mad crush on someone, will you be a wingman and help him get a date? Do you push your friends to succeed? Be the kind of person who fights to bring value to your friends if you want someone to be that kind of person for you. That's the only way either of you will deserve such a rad friend!

Here's the critical, important key: Crew members aren't envious of each other's successes and they aren't possessive. Instead, they celebrate each other's wins in life . . . simply because they care about one another. They're just plain stoked when their Battle Crewmate goes on a date, has a blast at a party, slays the math test, gets the lead role in the play, lands first chair in the band, wins the public speaking trophy . . . or whatever! They're excited for each other to succeed.

One of the coolest ways a friend can help to make you better is by encouraging you to find a coach who can help you to improve, or to perform at a higher level than they can. If somebody does that for you, that person sees your potential and wants you to reach it. And you know what? You can do that for your crew, too!

Another way crew members build each other up is by helping the other find more strength when he needs it. It could be spotting him through a bench press, sure. But it could also be giving him a great piece of advice or some encouragement in dark times. Sometimes you feel inspired just by who they are. Crew members build each other up to become better.

## Q2: HOW DOES THAT DUDE HAVE MY BACK?

Remember when Tommy Caldwell "dropped" his phone after the media circus started getting in Kevin's head? That's a perfect example of how a friend has a another friend's back. You, too, deserve friends who will have your back when you need them to. I'm talking about making sure that your Battle Crew looks out for you.

I'm not saying that you should demand that your friends smash their phones into a million tiny pieces to prove themselves worthy of your friendship. Instead, here are some other ways you can know that your friends have your back:

### THEY'RE WITH YOU THROUGH STORMS

You want friends who stick with you through the hard stuff.

Down in Arkansas, there's a small school called Lyon College. A few years ago, one of the football coaches there was diagnosed with cancer. In solidarity, each of the team members showed up at practice with his head shaved. Their coach's chemotherapy treatments caused him to lose his hair, so together, the team said to their coach, *We got your back. We're with you.*

A more everyday example: Let's say you're walking in your school's hallway and suddenly you overhear somebody trash-talking you. You stop dead in your tracks and you get mad or sad or scared. Either way, your heart sinks.

Then you hear another voice that you recognize. It's one of your friends! He interrupts the smack-talker and practically yells, "Hey, keep your mouth shut about my friend."

Wouldn't that feel awesome? To know that your friends defend you?

That's because you deserve friends who will stand up to someone who is talking smack about you. And remember, if you want friends who will have your back when you need them, you need to be that kind of person for them!

## THEY SEE YOUR STRENGTHS

Friends recognize what's awesome about each other and cheer each other on. Crew members respect each other because they know that the whole crew is stronger because of every person in it. Think of a rope: A rope isn't just a singular flimsy band. Instead, it works like friendships—it's made of many cords woven together, staying strong when one of you is holding a lot of weight. This is why an 11-millimeter climbing rope can hold 2,400 kilograms. That's 5,280 pounds, more than the weight of a Ford F150!

When you improve at something, a friend isn't intimidated or fearful of you outshining them. Can you imagine if Kevin was envious of Tommy for being the first to climb pitch 15 on the Dawn Wall? Or if Tommy was envious of Kevin for climbing it direct? If either of them was burning with envy, it would have eaten them up from the inside and nobody would have succeeded! Neither would've had the support he needed to do the thing they did.

## "CALLING YOU OUT" CAN BE HAVING YOUR BACK

Another way people can look out for you is by telling you what you need to hear and being honest with you, even if it's uncomfortable. A friend who will tell you what you need to hear—and who says it in a way that makes you know you're still supported—is an *amazing* friend.

What does that look like? It's when friends have the courage to say that their buds aren't acting with respect and integrity. It's pointing out that they aren't living by their Warrior Creeds. It's saying, "That's not cool," from a place of believing that somebody is better than their actions. It could be suggesting that a friend see a therapist or change their behaviors. It's not out of judgment, insult, or the intention to attack character. It's done in a caring way. It could even be a group intervention, where several people speak to someone out of love. Why? Because friends look out for their Battle Crews and the good of the larger tribe. That's what it means to have someone's back in a courageous way.

## THEY SUPPORT YOUR VALUES

A crew member doesn't need to have the exact same creed as you, but they do need to support the values you stand for. They respect the man you've chosen to be, and they don't threaten the values in your creed.

What if someone comes along and asks you to lie for them? Or suggests that you fry bugs under a magnifying glass? Or acts cruel in any way, to anyone? What if someone won't stop complaining and is negative all day, every day?

For me, a person like that doesn't get to be a part of my crew. Will I still be cool with them? Usually. But no matter what, nobody gets to be a part of my inner circle unless they support my values. They stay a part of the tribe, but they don't get to be a part of the Battle Crew.

I suggest you take a similar approach, because the energy-sucking drain that negative people will have on your success (and your potential for success) is totally not worth it. The small bit of discomfort it takes to set boundaries with life-draining people makes things so much easier in the long run. Don't get caught up in the drama of people you already know aren't going to support your values.

## Q3: DOES THAT DUDE RESPECT MY BOUNDARIES?

The last quality to look for in your Battle Crew members is that they respect you when you say no. Your crew honors your boundaries.

In fact, this is a major way that people prove they respect one another in general. If one dude can say no to something and fully trust that the other guy will say, "Okay, cool, no problem," they can be assured of respect. Gotta wash dishes, do homework, go on a date, or teach the cat to do backflips? "Cool, catch you next time" is what you should hear back! Sure, friends might give you a hard time because they want you around, like, "Bro, the snowboarding trip is gonna be epic! C'mon, you're gonna miss out!"—those are friends being good crew members. They're saying they want you around.

Along those lines, I can promise you there will come a day when you'll go to a party and you'll meet an aggressive drinker. This person will be practically forcing everyone around them to drink alcohol or drink it faster. That person doesn't respect other people. You included.

Real friends don't destroy their bodies together. Mutual self-destruction is a pretty flimsy standard to pick your friends by.

If you realize someone doesn't respect your boundaries, don't let them into your Battle Crew.

## WHAT TO DO NEXT

Your challenge is to start looking for these people! Eventually, you want to end up with about five people who can make you better, have your back, and respect your boundaries.

Aim to find a crew—or crews—wherever you spend a lot of your time. Find at least one crew member in school. This is your brain crew. Also find your activities and sports crews in your clubs and on your teams.

But most important, be sure to find your family crew. These are the people you can safely talk to about your feelings and what's going on inside. These could be your parents, siblings, grandparents, stepparents, a trusted adult, or a friend who is like a ninety-year-old Buddha of wisdom trapped in a kid's body.

When you're ready to start dating, or if you already are, your romantic partner should definitely pass the three-part crew check! Love interests become primary crew members for a lot of people. This person knows your heart, your spirit, and your body more intensely than anyone else. When it comes to choosing a crew member for life, you should *definitely* be able to say that person makes you better, has your back, and respects your boundaries.

Okay, amazing work, my friend! You've completed Challenge 5 and you're well over halfway through your training. You've got all the skills necessary for finding a Battle Crew for life! Follow these steps and you're going to be still hanging out with that crew years from now, just as Kevin Jorgeson and Tommy Caldwell still climb together!

It's also time to muster up some energy and some courage. You've got one challenge remaining before completing Phase II of your Warrior training! Do you have what it takes?

# TRAINING GROUNDS:
## FORM YOUR BATTLE CREW

### KNOW IT

Boys don't make an effort to be good friends to those in their lives. A True Warrior carefully builds a crew that promises to ensure each member becomes a better person, has each other's backs, and respects one another's boundaries.

### ACT ON IT

- Repeat the three-part crew check. What are the three qualifications that every person close to you must meet?

- Give yourself permission, right now, to NOT become close friends with anyone who doesn't pass the three-part crew member check. You don't need to be a jerk to anyone . . . but when you realize that someone drags you down more than they lift you up and there's no sign of that ever changing . . . please know that it's okay not to be friends with that person.

- Tell two to five people in your life who meet the three-part crew check that you would like to keep them close! Send them a text or a message to let them know how much you value and appreciate them!

# CHALLENGE 6: GET GRITTY

Yesterday is history,
tomorrow is a mystery,
but today is a gift.
That is why they call it the present.

## —MASTER OOGWAY,
### *KUNG FU PANDA*

# WORLD'S GREATEST FAILURE

You lick fatty bits of penguin from your beard. Your food supply of seal meat and penguins is running dangerously low. Every calorie counts out here. You and your twenty-seven crew members are hungry. So are your sixty-nine sled dogs, each weighing a hundred pounds.

It's been fourteen months since you and your crew left London on this expedition to the Antarctic. Then things went haywire when, nine months ago, your ship became wedged and then trapped in this enormous ice shelf. As temperatures dropped and ice grew around your floating home, every inch of your vessel's 141-foot-long underbelly became encased in the endless frozen expanse. During the blackness of winter, when light ceased to exist, it felt like being committed to a floating prison.

As you stand next to your ship, taking a turn out on the ice, you stare across the tundra. This epic iceberg is more like a continent, thirteen times larger than your home country of Ireland. The frigid air burns your lungs. Snow beneath your boots squeaks and crunches, protesting against your body weight. Beneath that snow is a solid sheet of ice that extends hundreds of miles in every direction

and, according to your crew's last measurement, it's eighteen feet thick.

Earlier this morning, you dispatched a hunting team. With any luck, they'll bring back a few more sleds of penguin meat. You're standing on the ice while you await their return. Beside you, the ship's captain, Frank Worsley, grimly measures the sun's position in the sky. He informs you that, over the past nine months that you've been trapped, the berg has carried your team hundreds of miles northeast, into the middle of the Weddell Sea.

All of a sudden, the slippery ice under-foot begins to shake like an earthquake. For a moment, you think the ice is open-ing. Then your heart drops down to your kneecaps.

"The ice is closing!" you yell, warning your men. "Off the boat!"

Two vise grips, each weighing 20 million tons, begin to crush your ship from both sides. The hull splinters open and slushy, freezing water gushes inside. Your expedition photographer starts filming just in time to capture footage of the two rear masts exploding like heavy fireworks. They splinter shards of wood onto the deck.

You know the *Endurance* is damaged beyond repair. It will sink—and with it, your sleeping quarters. You can salvage your supplies and three lifeboats . . . but this ship is your home!

With the ship now too dangerous to sleep in, you and your men will live out on the ice. As you begin searching for a suitable spot to build a camp, you say to Frank Wild, your right-hand man, "What the ice gets, the ice keeps."

For the next three and a half weeks, the abandoned *Endurance* stands her ground while pressure wave after pressure wave of the ice continent bashes into her belly. Finally, on November 21, 1915, you cry out, "She's going, boys!" The warming temperatures have caused the ice to swallow her into the darkness of the ocean.

Not a soul knows your location. There's zero chance of rescue and no way to radio for help. Everyone you know thinks you're on the other side of Antarctica by now—not drifting into the most dangerous sea in the world on a melting iceberg. You don't even have a ship. But what *do* you have? Dwindling food rations. Three wooden dinghies, sixty-nine dogs, and twenty-eight mouths to feed.

The embarrassment of yet another failure looms over you like a ghost. You already lost the title of being the first to reach the South Pole. After you failed twice, Norwegian explorer Roald Amundsen beat you to it. So you decided to be the first to travel *across* all of Antarctica. *Surely that'll cement my name as a great explorer,* you thought. You found a vessel with a six-foot-thick steel bow, making the *Endurance* a 141-foot-long battering ram.

After setting out from London, she spent seven months smashing through mile after mile of sea ice and made it within a hundred miles of Antarctica's shoreline. Now, nine months after that, you are without a ship, without a home, without options. You and your men sleep inside tents on top of the endless ice. You have barely enough to eat, and morale is dangerously low. You realize that there's no changing what's happened. Your only choice is to accept what is. And move forward.

You gather your crew and tell them their lives are more valuable than the expedition's original purpose. "Every man lives," you declare as the new purpose of the expedition, following it with "Today, men, today we'll go home."

Even in successful Antarctic expeditions, "no fatalities" is virtually unheard-of. That's why some believe your optimism to be foolish. To you, it's not optimism. You *have determination*. You don't know the exact plan, but you know you can innovate. You can adapt. You can invent solutions. You *know how to see better options*.

You order skis to be built for the three lifeboats out of salvaged wood from the ship. Each boat, stripped bare, weighs one ton. That's three tons, plus the weight of skis, food, cookware, your cast-iron stove, ammunition, rifles, tents, sleeping bags, and dog-sled equipment. You, your men, and the dogs will drag it all across the broken and cracked ice. All day. Every day. For months. Eventually, you'll reach the edge of your floating ice continent, and you'll need them for what comes next.

You set out and begin your journey. Soon it becomes apparent that your sixty-nine beloved dogs are too many mouths to feed. Your men are starving. Knowing there is no other choice, you order that they be shot. You and your distraught, starving men eat your beloved, loyal companions.

You forge on.

On one particularly dreary day of marching, a thirteen-foot-long leopard seal bursts through the ice and chases your crew member Thomas Ordes-Lee. The lethal predator is seconds away from having him for dinner, but Frank Wild shoots it dead. Knifing open the leopard seal's belly, you discover a collection of half-digested fish. *Fish!* The whole crew gobbles up the hijacked cod and silverfish. You feel relief for the first time in weeks.

After four and a half months of journeying on the ice, thirteen months after you began your mission, you realize that the thick, uniform ice is finally giving way to slush. It's time for the next phase of your journey. Starved and exhausted, your team lowers the three lifeboats into the sea. You and twenty-seven men pile into the 22.5-foot wooden rowboats. And you push off among the scattered, towering icebergs. As your crew pulls at the oars, you realize that your enemy has changed. No longer the endless white ice, it's now the black salty waters of the sea.

# ERNEST SHACKLETON: THE GRITTIEST MAN WHO EVER LIVED

Sir Ernest Shackleton and his crew failed their original mission by every measure. Crashing and sinking a ship before reaching the continent they were trying to cross meant the expedition was a colossal failure.

And Shackleton had already failed twice at reaching the South Pole! The man could never seem to accomplish what he set out to do. Yet he is remembered as one of the greatest explorers, survivors, and leaders of all time. His legendary story has been made into films, documentaries, books, and leadership case studies because of what he did after launching three rowboats into the Weddell Sea.

Each of the three wooden lifeboats was about the size of a shopping mall parking space. The sailors rowed them through an obstacle course of flipping, churning, calving, collapsing, and colliding icebergs. Each shift, roll, and turn of the ice chunks sent massive breaking waves toward their tiny boats.

They measured the tips of some of the bergs at hundreds of feet high. We now know that icebergs are 90 percent submerged. So if they saw a hundred feet of ice above the surface, that meant that nine hundred feet of unstable ice lurked below the surface. One small balance shift could cause the entire berg to start rolling, violently sucking them underwater.

During the nights, they hauled the boats ashore and slept on the flattest, most stable icebergs they could find. One evening, the ice cracked beneath a tent. Captain Ernest Holness, still in his sleeping bag, fell straight through the fissure and into a spine-chilling torrent of salt water! Shackleton, still awake and pacing restlessly, ran toward the splashing noise and yanked Holness and the bag out of the glacial river. Seconds later, with crushing force, the ice smashed back together, sealing shut the crack that the captain had fallen into.

Shackleton's every man lives theme was tested to the limits of human endurance. Food rations went down to one hot drink a day, plus a single dry, flaky biscuit. One man's advice was to "look at it for breakfast, suck at it for lunch, and eat it for dinner."

As they traveled farther from the pole, the bergs became too few and too small to sleep on. The men began to sleep in their lifeboats, roped together in a line, sterns tied to bows. One evening, humpback whales breached so close to their boats that, had one of the nine-ton sea mammals bumped into a boat or swum into a rope, all would have capsized and the men would have drowned.

After five days of rowing in the open sea, some men broke down and wept from the hunger, exhaustion, and brutal cold. It was too much to bear. Their freshwater barrels split open from cold and were contaminated by salt. Everyone had giant open blisters from the dehydration and relentless pounding of salty, icy water against their skin. They were piled on top of one another all day, every day. Nobody could tell whether their limbs were numb from the cold or from being pinned under the weight of another man's listless, blister-covered body.

After seven days at sea, and through a navigational miracle, they spotted lonely Elephant Island.

It was a grim landing. One man couldn't stand up to get himself out of the lifeboat. Nobody could summon the energy to celebrate. It had been a year and five months since they'd touched land. Some men buried their faces in the stones to convince themselves the earth was real. One man got an axe and started hacking at seals in a terrifying, hunger-fueled craze.

Only problem? Elephant Island is uninhabited. It's a beach lover's nightmare, made entirely of steep black cliffs and jagged glaciers with building-sized waves crashing into them. This devil's land is nowhere close to a shipping route, let alone civilization.

Storm after hurricane-force storm battered Shackleton's crew while they slept under the shelters of their overturned lifeboats on an icy, rocky island with a population of zero.

After four days of that, Shackleton decided there was no choice. He selected his five strongest sailors, and the six of them set off for South Georgia Island, over 800 miles away. If they made it, it would take them full circle, back to their last port of call before journeying toward the Antarctic. The other twenty-two men stayed on Elephant Island.

Captain Worsley again navigated by the sun's position in the sky. But now he had to take precise measurements while the tiny boat was being tossed by sixty-foot-tall waves. If Worsley miscalculated by a single degree, it would mean they'd veer sixty miles off course and miss the tiny fleck of land they were aiming for. Some waves were so tall and steep that when the crew rocketed toward their crests, the boat lost momentum. They'd then slip backward and, without a keel to keep them in a straight line, hurtle back down the face of the icy waves, surfing dangerously out of control.

It was so cold that their soaked clothing froze their bodies together. Often, they were too weak to pull themselves apart. But they still had to take turns submerging their frostbitten fingers under the Antarctic seawater in order to chisel away the ice forming on the boat's underbelly, threatening to sink it. One man was desperate for a sip of his water ration. He accidentally froze his cup to his upper lip and ripped it off.

On day sixteen, they finished one of the greatest sea crossings of all time, reaching South Georgia Island on May 20, 1916. They had set sail from the same island a year and a half prior. But now they were on the wrong side of the 1,450-square-mile earth lump in the ocean. The boat was too battered to continue sailing around it, so they were going to have to walk across it. Fortunately, the island is long and narrow, so it was "only" a twenty-seven-mile distance across. Two weren't even capable of trying. They stayed behind with a caretaker, desperately clutching to the last threads of their lives. Shackleton, Worsely, and Crean shoved nails and screws through their boots for traction. With no light except fortunate moonshine, they made a marathon-distance journey, traversing the glacier-covered island, replete with 3,000-foot cliffs. They had no tents, no sleeping bags, and maps that weren't even accurate. GPS devices and Clif bars didn't even exist. They had only a single tattered rope and a single pickaxe.

They were doing it on their final reserves of life, even though this land had never before been crossed in all of human history. They couldn't stop or they'd lose too much body heat and die from the cold. At one point, in the middle of the night, the three men had to sit on their coiled rope and use it as a sled to make their way down an 1,800-foot sheet of ice . . . with only the moon to light their way!

Finally, after marching for thirty-six hours, they rappelled down a three-hundred-foot-tall waterfall and stumbled like zombies into Stromness Bay, a whaling station. They looked so terrible that children ran away screaming in terror.

When the station manager heard their story, he immediately sent whalers to rescue the two men on the other side of the island. He said, "I have never heard of such a feat as rowing a 22.5-foot boat across 800 miles of the world's stormiest seas, then climbing a never-before-climbed mountain range. These are men."

Being called a man wasn't good enough for Shackleton. He hadn't yet reached his true finish line. *Every man lives.*

Day and night he worked to rescue his twenty-two crew members left behind on Elephant Island. He attempted three separate voyages on three separate ships, but each time he was blocked by sea ice. It had been four months since they waved goodbye to him! The crew figured Shackleton was either dead or drinking lemonade on a beach somewhere.

Yet Shackleton persisted "with grit and spirit." On the fourth voyage to the island, all remaining twenty-two men were finally rescued. After being gone for twenty-four months and twenty-two days, *everyone went home.*

# WHO'S MANLIER?

Sir Ernest Shackleton could be the grittiest man who ever lived. If you think Tough Mudder races sound hard, try doing what Shackleton and his men did.

Once, when they desperately needed food, THEY LASSOED A WHALE WITH A ROPE. Then they knotted the rope to their boat and played tug-of-war *with a whale.* And they won!

But let me ask you something: Is it more manly to row a whale home for dinner—or launch over the Great Wall of China on a skateboard?

It's a trick question. Neither is more manly than the other.

It doesn't actually matter whether you think that being a man means getting a face tattoo or letting ants eat your hands. It doesn't matter if you decide that Navy SEAL training is the thing for you or if you realize you're more of an Army Ranger kinda guy. If you believe that being a man means standing up for LGBTQ rights, planting a million trees, starting your own business, or playing a flute to a cactus while your cat finally does backflips—it's ALL manly so long as you do it with one thing:

Grit.

To hear Shackleton tell it, it's grit that makes a man a hero, not the specifics of his story.

Grit is how you can inspire your tribe to endure, to keep on, to be at their best, and to step up their game. Just by having grit, you can inspire the rest of us to want to become as awesome as possible. Literally, the definition of *inspire* is "to breathe life into."

So, what does it take to be so rad that you breathe life into other people and help them make it through the worst conditions known to humankind? How do you become a life-giving man? An inspiring person? How do you thrive?

You succeed at Challenge 6.

**Challenge 6 is to get gritty! That means to have the traits that will help you to press on when you're not sure you can press on. It doesn't mean, in this moment, having everything that you'll need for everything you'll ever face in life. No, to succeed, you only need to know three questions that will help you move through any challenging moment in the future.**

# THE COMPONENTS OF GRIT

I looked up synonyms for *grit*. Check out what's in a thesaurus: To have grit is to have "courage" and "resolve." It's to have "character."

"Nerve," "valor," "moral fiber," "determination," "hope," and "endurance" are all in there. But the most laughable definition in a thesaurus? It said it means to have "balls." Yeah, go show your English teacher for a laugh (and maybe detention).

That's a lot of words. So here's what matters for Warriors. Grit is three things: Presence, Determination, and Options. Shackleton inspired his Battle Crew to survive because he had these three ingredients. Take on these traits and you'll be able to endure through anything!

## GRIT, COMPONENT #1: PRESENCE

Sir Ernest Shackleton came to accept reality and live in the now after his ship, his crew's home, sank through a melting iceberg.

You know what I'd have done? I would have told myself how badly I'd screwed up. I'd have thought of all the mistakes we'd made. I'd have started freaking out, worrying about what we were going to do when the ice melted. *When the ammunition runs out, what will we eat? When the tents collapse, where will we sleep? How will we navigate without the sun?* I'd have beaten myself up about what happened in the past and I'd have been anxious about what was going to happen in the future.

Instead, one of the first things Shackleton said to his men when the *Endurance* sank was "Today, men, today we go home."

He accepted his present reality. He didn't whine about what had already happened. He didn't have a panic attack about what might happen months into the future. *He was right there, with his crew, in the moment.*

That's why his men felt inspired and loyal all at once. He focused on what was here and now, within his control.

### HOW MANY BRAIN TABS DO YOU HAVE OPEN?

Maybe you're like me, and when you're online, you've got 45 internet tabs open. I usually can't find what I'm looking for and I get distracted by something, and next thing I know, I'm watching a video of someone's cat doing backflips.

Sound familiar?

Well, our brains also have open "tabs"! We are trying to keep track of so many things that we rarely get to enjoy the tab that's open!

Presence is the rarest gift we have to give to another person. Giving undivided attention, completely showing up in the moment, being *with* someone in human interactions—not just physically with them, but mentally and emotionally, fully *there*. That's how we connect with other human beings.

So how can you become more present so that there's a chance for a spark with people? There are three very easy ways to get started:

First, deny your cyborg existence. You know what I think is the creepiest thing ever? It's lifting your head up from technology and seeing how many human beings are living like they're cyborgs.

Don't misunderstand: Technology is not inherently evil, any more than a pencil eraser is evil. Technology is just a tool. You just gotta be sure it makes your life better and doesn't remove you from the living! The question you gotta constantly ask yourself is: "Am I using this technology or is this technology using me?"

If it's using you, then get back to living in the present reality.

Second, accept your situation. How many live sports games, concerts, hikes, sunsets would be enjoyed infinitely more if people started accepting the reality of where they actually are instead of being distracted?

How many dinners would become connective experiences and

wonderful memories if we started choosing to participate in meal-time conversations?

How many brokenhearted people would be free to be happy if they finally accepted that, for example, their ex doesn't actually want to see them again? If they accepted their current situation, they might actually get what they want in the end . . . someone who loves them.

It sounds kind of "no duh," but this is an epic problem. The next time you're at a restaurant or a game or a concert, look around. How many people do you see who are not actually *there*? Notice who's on their phones and ignoring the very people they're with. Notice who's zoning out and staring out a window. Instead of judging those people, ask yourself, "When do I do that same exact thing?"

Finally, drop the front and be real. The last trick for becoming more present is to be real about what's going on inside you. This does not mean spill your deepest, darkest secrets to anybody and everybody. It means be completely honest about your feelings and what you're going through. Quit trying to have a mask of toughness or niceness, and instead be authentic. That's being real.

When something is bothering you, talk about it with the person who's bugging you. Don't invent ideas about what they may or may not be thinking. Don't complain to other people who have nothing to do with the situation. That's what boys do. Just bring it up with the actual person and work it out, setting healthy boundaries with each other. That's being real. That's what men do.

## GRIT, COMPONENT #2: DETERMINATION

In every new impossible scenario, Shackleton essentially said to himself and his crew: "It will work. We'll make it work. We'll get there no matter what."

When Shackleton, Worsley, and Second Officer Tom Crean finished climbing across South Georgia Island and reached the whaling station, Worsley said to Shackleton, "Boss, I had a curious feeling on the march that there was another person with us."

Crean chimed in and agreed; he also thought they were four.

Shackleton answered them, "So did I." He even journaled about it: *When I look back on those days, I have no doubt that Providence guided us, not only across those snow fields, but across the storm-white sea that separated Elephant Island from our landing-place.*

These aren't particularly religious men. But to leave this out would be to cheat you of the full story.

The truth about Providence or God or the universe or It, though, is hard to argue with: When you have an unstoppable resolve to make something happen, when you will not quit no matter what obstacles come your way, and when you refuse to back down on your journey to your true finish line, then somehow, without explanation, and when you least expect it, miracles start to happen.

This is why one of my favorite African proverbs is "When you pray, move your feet." It means: When you ask for something, do something. Start taking steps to make it happen!

Determination is the trait that Shackleton relied on to get all his men to row in the same direction and accomplish their impossible objective. Often, he didn't know what the next step in his plan was. But he endured nearly two years of spirit-crushing trials because he was determined to succeed.

Your willpower and commitment are like the battery banks for your life. That's where you draw your energy from! Bruce Lee, one of the greatest martial artists of all time, said, "You must have complete determination. The worst opponent you can come across is one whose aim has become an obsession. For instance, if a man has decided that he is going to bite off your nose no matter what happens to him in the process, the chances are he will succeed in doing it. He may be severely beaten up, too, but that will not stop him from carrying out his objective. That is the real fighter."

## GRIT, COMPONENT #3: INGENUITY

During the entire journey, Shackleton filtered everything through one question: "How do I get these men home?"

Finding the answer required that Shackleton's crew be able to creatively find solutions where few others would be able to. That's because the last component of grit is ingenuity. That's another word for seeing better options. For example, before the *Endurance* sank, the chef tore out parts of the ship's engine and made them into a portable stove. *Ingenious!*

Each day, Shackleton created a plan and an alternate plan, but he was also flexible when the plan and the alternate plan went haywire. He always chose to spot solutions instead of obstacles.

Ingenuity means using your inventiveness and creativity to solve problems. It's knowing that there's always a solution—you just have to figure out what it is.

This is why Lao Tzu said, "Water is the softest thing, yet it can penetrate mountains and earth. This shows clearly the principle of softness overcoming hardness. . . . What is more malleable is always superior over that which is immovable."

When Shackleton's team first put their lifeboats into the water, their original plan wasn't even to travel to Elephant Island. In fact, while they were at sea, their plan changed four separate times! As expedition leader, he stayed flexible because change is the only thing in life that will always be there.

True statistic from the Bureau of Labor Statistics: The average person holds twelve jobs in their lifetime. You know what this means? It means that most adults still don't know what they want to be when they grow up!

That also means it's okay for YOU to not know what you want to be when you grow up, too! You don't need to know the exact path that your entire life is going to take. Just because everybody has been asking, "What do you want to be when you grow up?" since you could first talk, you don't have to actually know!

Is it good to think about those things? Yeah, of course! But all you've really gotta be able to do is to be creative, to innovate, and to adapt.

I told you about my Green Beret buddy, Steve Hemmann. Well, here's another one of his bits of wisdom. He said that when he was in high school, he didn't know what he wanted to do. All he knew for sure was that he wanted to find something that would push him mentally, spiritually, physically, and socially in the most challenging environment possible. He believed that's what it would take to bring out his best.

After looking at all the options, he decided that West Point, the United States' premier military academy, was the place for him.

When he first got there, he didn't know that there was such a thing as Army Ranger training. He didn't even know the difference between being an "officer" and being "enlisted." He didn't start with the creed memorized, and he couldn't apply a choke hold or raid a building with heavy artillery.

He was just drawn to what he personally saw as the most badass and intense thing that he could undergo. So he adapted to each new challenge as he went, and when something presented itself that he didn't know how to handle, he treated it as an opportunity to bring out something even more badass from within.

Having options doesn't mean not taking one. It means studying them all and thinking critically. Then, after they're all laid out on the table and several look good, *that's* when you follow the nudge of your instincts. Often, there are multiple great options and you've just got to go with your gut and pick one.

Like famous mountaineer Ed Viesturs says, "Your instincts are telling you something. Trust them and listen to them."

## THREE GRITTY QUESTIONS

You can ask yourself three questions to embrace all three of these traits.

**The first question makes you present:**
*What can I do to be more "here"?*

**The second question gets at your determination:**
*How deep is my willpower?*

**The third question calls on your ingenuity:**
*What options exist that I haven't seen yet?*

Find yourself stuck in any life situation? Ask those three questions and you'll get gritty in no time flat! Learn to ask those three questions when you face anything tough in your life and you will succeed at Challenge 6. (Let's just hope it doesn't involve eating penguins!)

# TRAINING GROUNDS:
## GET GRITTY

### KNOW IT

Boys give up, create drama, and have self-pity when things don't go according to plan. A True Warrior tackles life problems with presence, determination, and ingenuity.

### ACT ON IT

☐ The next conversation you have, ask yourself, "How can I be more fully 'here' and present with this person?" You might put away your phone or decide to ask some awesome questions . . . but your task is to ask yourself how you can be "there" with the next human you interact with.

☐ Which class in school do you sometimes feel like giving up on? C'mon, I know there's one! Okay, now, ask yourself: "How deep do my determination and willpower go?" Simply by asking that, you'll find the resolve to press on!

☐ Think about a problem in your life. Do you know why it's there? That problem exists because you haven't discovered a better option for dealing with it. So instead of thinking about "that thing" as a problem, think of it as the world's way of asking: "What better options exist for handling your problem?"

# ACHIEVEMENT UNLOCKED! LEVEL II COMPLETE!

When you like a flower,
you just pluck it.
But when you love a flower,
you water it daily.

—GAUTAMA BUDDHA

# CONGRATULATIONS, WARRIOR! YOUR DEFENSES ARE UPGRADED!

Look at you go! You learned how to set boundaries when you escaped from a communist country. Then you formed a Battle Crew when you crushed the world's hardest rock climb. Last but not least, you proved your grit when you casually threw in a little Antarctic rescue operation. You're no longer fighting just for the sake of fighting. You're the kind of human who will throw down for peace and to protect people. The best kind of human.

Before we enter the last phase of your training, there's one more candid conversation you've earned. And if you've legitimately passed every challenge up till now, you're more of a man than most males out there. I don't say that so you can brag. I say it because that's why I think you're ready to talk, man-to-man, about what's really going on when it comes to dating, relationships, and . . . yes, sex.

## WHEN DO WE TALK ABOUT SEX, DUDE?

If you've hit puberty, then at some point while reading this book, you have had a sexual thought. And if you're not there yet, you will be one day, and for now you are exactly where you should be. No matter the stage of your development, no matter your gender or sexual orientation, there's no way around it: Sexuality is a big part of being human.

It's *such* a big part of our humanity that, if you're going to become an independent man who can protect your tribe, then you *have* to understand how sex and your sexuality affect you and the people around you. It's impossible to talk about being a man without talking about sex.

You may be ready to start thinking about dating, physical affection, and your sexuality. You may have zero interest in those things. You may not even know what those words mean! Wherever you're at, that's okay. What I firmly believe is that every person around your age needs to feel comfortable understanding and talking about the way their body works. Talking about sex should be a conversation that's open, clear, and void of shame or judgment.

I know, though. This subject makes some people uncomfortable. And you might be one of those people. If so, trust me: coming from a religious background, I definitely get it. But denying reality and keeping hush-hush about something that is literally responsible for our earthly existence is not the answer.

What I highly recommend to you is this: talk about this chapter, and this aspect of yourself, with an adult you trust, like, and respect. There's no reason for any shame, embarrassment, or weirdness here.

For most guys, sex education is an unfortunate and not super-enlightening one or two weeks in a classroom, an even more awkward one-time talk with parents, followed by confusing and often completely incorrect info from friends, and then pornography. For something that the average eighteen-to-twenty-four-year-old male thinks about 34.2 times a day, I'd say that's entirely unhealthy.

Soon you'll be in that eighteen-to-twenty-four age range and a physically grown male. But if you want to be a man, you have to know what to do with pressures that will build, both literally in your body and in the culture you're a part of.

If you're not thinking about sex yet, this stuff might sound strange. Again, that's okay, and even more of a reason to read this chapter with a trusted adult. If you choose to do that, have them check out this special section I wrote just for them.

TRUSTED ADULTS AND CONFIDANTES: Think back to how old you were when you first wondered about what sex meant. Or what it looked like. Or felt like. Whatever your experience, studies show that today's kids become curious about these subjects three to four years earlier than the average adult thinks is true. For boys, that's most frequently between the ages of seven and eleven.

Questions about sexuality at this age are healthy questions about the reality of life. That's why having frequent and non-judgmental conversations about sex, dating, consent, pornography, and toxic character traits will help teens and preteens get accurate answers about what they're already wondering about.

It's a no-brainer: pretending that preteens aren't thinking about their developing sexuality will result in conversational voids. Nature abhors a vacuum, and without openly discussing these subjects, young people will fill in the gap with a litany of incorrect hearsay and online misinformation (aka porn).

That's why this chapter approaches this subject directly. It's a launching point for discussion. Yet there is no one-size-fits-all when it comes to this stuff. That's why I'm counting on you to walk through the wide-open door I'm giving you here. Use this chapter to start real, honest, and recurring discussions with the young adults in your life about your opinions, beliefs, and understandings about each of these subjects.

So, if you're somebody who has questions about sex, I'm here to give you some straight-talkin' answers. Because even harder than talking about sex is learning about it. Especially learning about what a *healthy* sexual relationship looks like. In this part of your training, there's no actual challenge, no checklist of achievements, and definitely no bullet ant stings. (CAN YOU IMAGINE?) That's because, with sex, no challenge, quest, or checklist should ever be involved. You're also not going to get someone else's unbelievable, larger-than-life story, because sex and sexuality are not about living up to anyone else's standards.

Can you also look to your parents and adults in your life for guidance on this stuff? Yes, absolutely! You should! But at the end of the day, how you approach romance is *entirely your choice*. Who you share your body with is a choice that is ONLY between you and that person. But it's a BIG choice. And understanding your own desires and interests—and how they line up with another person's—is no small feat. Let alone navigating some of the very real consequences of these decisions. That's why we're going to talk about what's real.

Look, I trust you're going to figure out what does what, what's called what, and what goes where without my help. Which is why, instead of an anatomy lesson, this section is about how to connect with people as people, at the same time you're discovering your sexuality and what turns you on.

I mean, how do you figure out what you want, what you like, and what pace you wanna go? And once you figure that out, assuming you find a cool person to share that with, how do you learn about what they want, what they like, and what pace they wanna go? This is important because when the day comes that you're ready to act on your sex drive, you absolutely MUST understand that it involves another person.

Read it again. Another *person*.

Not what's between their legs. Not even hair or eyes. You're not dealing with a collection of body parts and features. You're dealing with a person who has every right to their thoughts, emotions, and human rights, just like you. And they have a sex drive—and a set of values—all of their own. And another person's sex drive is, with 100 percent certainty, going to be different from yours.

The first part of that is understanding yourself.

# UNDERSTANDING YOURSELF

The initial stage of getting to know your sexuality is noticing what your thoughts and physical urges are telling you about what you want and who you want. Don't feel bad about paying attention to those things. And don't even act, yet, on what you're noticing. Just start by recognizing it for what it is. It's exactly the same as Challenge 2: you're becoming self-aware!

You've got to learn to notice when your sex drive shows up in your thoughts and in your body. That will give you a better understanding of what's going on, on your end (err . . . front end). By understanding how your body works, you're much more likely to not accidentally get carried away and take things in a direction that you—or the other person—aren't ready for.

How do you do that? You name it. Just say, "Ah yes, that's my sex drive talking." You can even use our other two intel strategies (body scan, watch your breath) to become aware of what's going on with you.

Here's what's real: If you notice your sexuality is becoming a bigger part of your identity, and especially if you find yourself wanting to do something about it, then this chapter is one billion percent for you. And if that's not you, that's okay, too. This stuff also applies to you. The pressure from your friends and the pressures in your body are not what make choices for you. You make choices for yourself. So if you want to wait until you're married to share your sexuality with someone else, that's also totally fine. Everything that's here will still hold true.

Here's the key: for hand-holding, dating, kissing, touching, and even when you're ready to have sex, *move at a pace that's right for you*. Although it doesn't often feel this way, there is zero rush to make anything happen. Be 100 percent certain that you're not acting on anyone's timeline except your own. Don't let anyone pressure or shame you into moving faster than your boundaries say you're ready for. It's not up to your friends, or movies, or siblings, or family to make decisions about your body. And whatever values you agree with—whether inspired by your culture or background or religion or parents or life experience or media—if they're genuinely true to you, then those are the values *you* should follow. That's your choice alone.

# BECOMING SEXUALLY SELF-AWARE

Truthfully? Most human beings first explore their sexuality by masturbating. Let's just settle this right now: Playing with yourself doesn't cause infertility, it won't make your penis fall off, you won't go blind, you definitely can't give yourself a sexually transmitted infection, and you don't have to worry about any of the other silly myths, either. I don't think masturbation makes you a bad person, and I don't think it means you're going to hell (if you believe there's a hell). I believe that your body is yours, and you have a right to feel pleasure.

Some people disagree with my opinion, and if you're one of them, that's okay. So let's stick to what's true: By the age of seventeen, 80 percent of boys have masturbated.

Also true: Orgasms are good for humans. There's no other way to say it. They reduce stress, anxiety, and depression. They improve sleep, which in turn improves focus. They improve immune function and reduce the chance of diabetes. For women, they also improve pelvic floor health.

But this does not mean you should lock yourself in the bathroom until you're forty years old, calling it "diabetes prevention," okay?

When that future day comes when you think, *Hey, I'm ready to really connect—in a way that includes being physical—with this other human being . . .* what then?

# THE RISKS ASSOCIATED WITH SEX

If you're considering having sex, there are risks you have to be prepared for. With sex comes the possibility of sexually transmitted infections (STIs) and pregnancy if you're with a girl. Protection, like condoms, should be used properly and 100 percent of the time. But there is always a degree of risk involved, even if you use a condom, as they are not 100 percent effective. If you're not ready or willing to accept those risks, then that's completely okay! Deciding to not have sex at all is called abstinence. Abstinence is a valid choice. Bottom line: if you're not prepared to deal with the possible consequences of sex, then you're not ready to have it.

That's what leads us to this critically important point: Physical connection can be an amazing thing when there's a real connection between two mature people. When it comes to hand-holding, cuddling, making out, touching, heavy petting, and sex, they all have this in common: those things can be off-the-charts awesome when the conditions are right.

But is it gonna be perfect every single time? No. Are there

gonna be weird, uncomfortable moments? Definitely. Is it possible that the two of you might have a physical connection and one or both people don't have a heart connection to match? Yes, absolutely.

That stuff happens.

That's what makes this point so critically important: trying to create a physical connection—on any level—without a baseline foundation of respect, understanding, and connection . . . takes this thing that can be *freaking incredible* and turns it into something awkward and uncomfortable. For everyone.

Physical touch alone will, with 100 percent certainty, NOT create a heart connection between two people. It doesn't work like that. But when you already have the connection and then you bring that to physical touch . . . dude. It is mind-blowingly amazing.

So how do you create that heart connection first? *You love people in action.*

# LOVING IN ACTION

I know what you're thinking: *C'mon, man, gimme the good stuff! Gimme the pickup lines, the "you won't believe what happened next" stories!*

Bummer for you, bro. I'm not gonna do that.

Besides, those are gimmicks. They're not authentic. They rely on charm, not connection. But I will give you something I've discovered to be a massive turn-on for people, in like, the weirdest and most surprising way. You're gonna roll your eyes, but I am absolutely not kidding. Here it is: boundaries.

Very hot.

You know how they say confidence is attractive? Well, look . . . if you get Legendary-level boundaries with your romantic partners, I swear on my life, it makes this totally unexpected vibe that's like, *Oooh, he's confident, he knows what he wants, and he's not scared to ask for it. That's attractive!*

Whether it's saying that you don't text after nine p.m., or you're not ready to be physical, or you need solo time with just your friends—setting boundaries is critical. It not only helps you stay aligned with your Warrior Creed, it's also attractive.

But to actually do that? You've gotta get to the connection part. Because the point of dating isn't about being seen with a hottie you're excited about. It's not about receiving high fives from your buddies, and it's definitely not about using your romantic partner to soothe your loneliness.

Love is not a feeling. Love is an action. It's something you do.

*What else, man?! I know you're holding back—gimme the good stuff on dating! Gimme a line, man, an actual sentence to say!*

Okay, okay, you got me.

As a dude who has dated some wonderful human beings, here's the absolute best line I've learned:

You say, "Hey, what makes you feel most _____?"

And then you add in what you want to know. You can add "happy" or "loved" or "cared for." You could add "angry" or "disrespected." You ask what you're genuinely curious about that makes them feel X.

And then do you know what you do next?

*Yo! Are you paying attention?*

What you do next is you *listen*. You learn about that person. Like, put every bit of yourself there, present, in the moment, in their shoes, trying to understand the human being you're talking to.

If you're picking up what they're putting down, you can then start acting on what they're saying! Because when you meet someone you're into, it's kinda dumb to do the things for them that make *you* feel loved. You gotta do the things for them that make *them* feel loved.

Think about it: The *only* way you can actually express your feelings to another person is *by what you do* to show them how you feel. For friends, parents, siblings, teachers, acquaintances, and lovers alike: You can express that you care for these people by making *them* feel loved. It's to actually *love them*. As a verb. As something you do.

# THIS IS YOUR BRAIN ON . . .

Hang on for a sec while I bring this to a different key for a moment. 'Cause reality is, even if you like what I'm saying, for a lot of guys, something gets in the way of love and hooking up and connection. And that's porn. And we gotta talk about it.

If you just squirmed, be cool, man. We're gonna leave emotions out of it and just cover some facts.

The vast majority of boys first see pornography when they are between eight and twelve years old. If you're like 93 percent of boys under eighteen, you've seen or used porn in some form.

Most of us see porn the first time when a friend shows us something or when we accidentally click on a weird web link. Usually? We're just curious to learn about sex. Psychologist Michael C.

Reichert says that "given the vacuum surrounding the topic of sex, boys find pornography the easiest way to learn about it."

Let me loosely summarize the rest of what he says about porn in his book: *If porn is how we're learning about sex, then what are we learning about sex from porn?*

*We are learning that it's theatrics. A performance without regard to the human you're interested in. Zero integrity.*

Get this: there was a legit experiment done a decade ago by a guy named Dr. William Struthers, who proved this point. He's got a PhD in biopsychology, which means he knows more than nearly anyone about how our brains control our thoughts, feelings, and behaviors.

Here's what he did: He made a bunch of cardboard butterflies, and they were super-sexy cardboard butterflies. I mean, I don't *personally* think the butterflies were sexy, but Struthers figured out what male butterflies are into and made fake cardboard female butterflies with all the features he'd discovered that male butterflies are into, and then he exaggerated those features.

The male butterflies went *wild*. They were like, *Ooh, baby, I could stare at the spots on your wings all day* sorta thing. The fake female butterflies were bigger and brighter than real-life female butterflies, which made the males do all sorts of unspeakable butterfly things to the exaggerated cardboard females.

Here's where this gets kinda sad. Struthers then introduced living, breathing, wing-flapping female butterflies to the males. Lots of them. The men could finally have a real-life antenna-rubbing relationship!

But even when real-life females were present, the males wouldn't stop trying to get it on with the fake cardboard butterflies! Their little butterfly brains had been hijacked. Literally, their brains were rewired so that they were only attracted to the impossibly exaggerated butterflies. They lost the ability to connect with real, flesh-and-bug-guts females.

Now, let's say you're like many people in America who believe that porn is harmless or that it's even healthy. After having a nice chat with Struthers about the mating habits of butterflies, go ahead and listen to Dr. Lawrence Tucker, a psychiatrist and neurologist. He put a bunch of eighteen-year-old pornography addicts into an MRI machine and scanned their brains. Now, a normal human brain is generally smooth and round. But a pornography addict's brain? It looks much more like the brain of a cocaine addict than the brain of a healthy human. This is why pornography addiction is "every bit as real as a drug addiction," says the documentary *Brain Heart World,* where this study is recorded in detail.

You might say, "Well, who cares what my brain looks like? It's covered by my skull." If you have this thought, it means your brain is having a serious problem telling you what your brain is for. If you physically alter your brain, you will change everything about your body's functions, your thoughts, and your relationships.

## HOW PORN CONTROLS YOUR BODY

Remember how the butterflies weren't interested in having relationships? Something similar happens in our human brains. In fact, never before in human history has getting an erection been a problem for human males in their teens. Yet watching pornography is linked with not being able to make things work down there. Porn causes a heart-penis disconnect. That's because when watching it, you are literally watching a performance. And if your understanding of sex is that it's a show, that doesn't make for healthy sex. Also, it puts all the focus on you alone and seriously diminishes the connection and respect that's needed between two people.

## HOW PORN CONTROLS YOUR RELATIONSHIPS

*Wait, whaaaa? I thought pornography would teach me about sex. I thought it would make me more skilled for when I'm physically intimate. I thought this was just people expressing their sexuality. It's free speech, right? I thought it wasn't a big deal. . . .*

Porn reduces people to parts. You're shown an edited, exaggerated image, and when you've had enough, you can click a button and that person just goes away. That's a perfectly acceptable way to treat an object, but not a person.

Yet with porn, that's how you're learning to view sex. Porn wires your brain to think that you're better than someone else, that they're an object to be used. Porn eliminates the human connection, the emotions, the intimacy, the tenderness, the spiritual warmth that are a part of really good sex. Too much porn, especially when you're young, can warp your idea of what's normal and what's desirable. Author Dr. Michael C. Reichert says that's the thing about porn that gives guys an "unrealistic view of what sex and intimacy are supposed to be." You will start to "find it difficult to get aroused by a real-life partner" because your brain is being given a fake map of how human relationships work.

Like butterflies trying to boink cardboard, your brain will start to prefer the exaggerated, fake version of intimacy on a screen. You'll be annoyed that real people are not available 24/7 and that they are more complex beings than actors in a video. And remember, once you view sex as something you perform, you'll want to know: "How'd I do? Did I impress you with that move?" And that's never what sex should be about.

# WHAT TO DO ABOUT PORN

If this doesn't sound like a future you want to opt into, you can start by setting boundaries for yourself. You can remove your own stumbling blocks by saying, "No phones in the bathroom" or "No screens in the bedroom." You can decide, "I'm not the kind of person who watches pornography" and "I prefer human relationships to a screen."

Better, you can have honest, real conversations with trusted mentors, your parents, and even your friends. You can break the silence surrounding porn simply by talking about it with people you trust. It's critical that we talk about it, because when our mistakes and problems are shameful to talk about, they can easily turn into addictions.

If you're curious to learn about what healthy sex is like, then here's a question you can start asking (to totally trustworthy adults): "What is healthy sex like?"

# WITH SEX, ARE MEN THE PROBLEM?

You may have heard the phrase "toxic masculinity." You may be wondering, does that phrase mean that all people who are masculine are toxic? Like, are we all bad people simply by being born men?

First off, to say that men are toxic simply because we are male is sexist. It's no more right to say that men are bad and women are good than the other way around. We are equal. And it is safe, acceptable, and desirable for you to be who you are, just as you are.

If you think of yourself as a man, male, or masculine, that is in no way bad, harmful, or toxic. You do not need to be embarrassed by your masculine edge.

We aren't toxic just for being men, but we do each have to understand how, purposefully or accidentally, men have historically been part of the problem that has led to the concept of "toxic masculinity." My hope here is that, going forward, you will be part of the solution.

There was a time in my life when I was definitely a part of the problem. At times, I still am. I've laughed at jokes I'm now embarrassed by. I've said and done things that I'm now mortified by. Sometimes I thought these things were just what guys did or that they were no big deal. Any of those sound familiar? They're how we end up hurting people in ways that *are* a big deal.

Fortunately, if toxic masculinity is a thing, then so is thriving masculinity.

There's a way that men can be at our best. Men can be lifegiving. We can be also lifesaving. Masculine men, at their finest, can bring out the best in themselves and in the people around them. A man can choose to live in his strength, his courage, his decisiveness, and he can use those qualities to improve the experience of every living thing he interacts with.

Unfortunately, that's not what many men choose. Which is why there's an entire movement built around asking men to choose differently.

# THE #METOO MOVEMENT

If you're going to be a man in today's culture, you need to know about #MeToo and what it means for you.

Here's how it started: Beginning in 2016, celebrities, politicians, and prominent business owners were publicly called out for abusing their power and taking advantage of people, sexually. Most of the accused abusers were male. And most of the victims were female.

It soon became clear that this wasn't just a problem of bigwigs abusing their power. It was happening on nearly every level of our culture: in schools, churches, workplaces, and even in families.

#MeToo is the movement that has begun to make it safer for survivors to speak up when they have been sexually harassed, abused, assaulted, raped, or taken advantage of.

A real man's response to the #MeToo movement should not be to cower and hide and wonder, *Gee whiz, who's gonna go down next?* That's weak. Cowering and waiting is what boys do. If we do that, it proves that we still haven't heard the message of the movement. Which, from my perspective, is the fact that survivors asked for an apology *in the form of a changed culture.*

An apology is not an apology unless we also change our actions. That's why a real man's response to the #MeToo movement is to step up and become a better man. It's to look honestly at how we've been a part of the problem. It's to start calling out our friends when they're being a part of the problem. I understand that you're not in the generation of men who contributed to what happened leading up to #MeToo. I understand that you may have done nothing to add to the problem. And that's why it's so important for you to know what happened in the past, because you have the potential to change *everything*. The #MeToo movement is asking us to up our game when we define what it means to be masculine. #MeToo asks us to make things like accountability, respect, and humanity our baseline standards, not things we aspire to. Women don't need to be saved. They *do* need to be seen as human beings who have as much worth as men—because they do, plain and simple.

You have the power to create real change in our world. You can make that difference by starting to listen.

Personally, one thing I hear women asking us is to see through their eyes.

What about you? What are you hearing?

# HOW WE DEHUMANIZE WOMEN

From the get-go in life, boys are shamed into thinking that any traits considered feminine should be avoided at all costs. Everything from how we throw a ball to how we dress to how deep our voices are to whether we cry . . . it's all shaped by the toxic message that, if we're "like a woman" in any way, we are losers.

That's not an exaggeration. Gender-equality advocate Tony Porter once asked a male student athlete, "What would you say if your coach called you a girl in front of all of your teammates?" The kid said, "It would destroy me." He believed that being equal to a girl would be the end of his existence. That's internal messaging that makes us think that women are less than us.

These messages are everywhere. Have you ever wondered why

we call someone a "mama's boy" when we consider him wimpy? The message we're downloading, without even realizing it, is *If I don't do risky and dumb things that could kill me, and if I need any help or support from a woman, I guess I'm weak.*

This is messed up, because it also makes guys think it's bad to have any traits that we consider "feminine," like compassion, tenderness, and warmth. It also brainwashes us into believing that girls can't be tough or take risks. This is how we create the false, toxic message that straight males are superior humans. This garbage message in our culture makes women less than men.

We also have a similar message about gay people. We say "Don't be gay" when you think to give your buddy a hug or lean on a guy's shoulder when you're hanging out (and that's me going easy on the language). Without a doubt, you hear much more insulting stuff when it comes to queerness.

Is this kind of talk really protecting your tribe?

The good news is that a lot of guys ARE getting it. They are courageously speaking up. If you're one of them, you have a lot to be proud of. You are protecting your tribe.

# HOOKING UP IS LIKE SKYDIVING

In 2014, Google executive Alan Eustace completed one of the most amazing stunts of all time. Suspended facedown from a helium balloon, he was pulled up into the sky for two hours until he reached 135,890 feet above sea level. He was four and a half Everests high, in a space suit, far above Earth, in the stratosphere. The curvature of the Earth was visible beneath him.

Alan mentally reviewed his safety checks. He asked ground control, "Is everyone ready?"

"Yes," came the answer.

Then came the countdown.

5—4—3—2—1 . . .

That's when Alan started free-falling. He spent fourteen minutes falling through the stratosphere at 822 miles per hour after breaking the sound barrier, tumbling end over end toward the earth.

Skydiving done right looks like that. Everyone clearly communicated that they were ready. That's how the best of the best do it, and that's how Alan's world-record-setting skydiving jump went down—with everybody clearly on board.

*That* is how you want to go about getting physical with someone else.

Just like skydiving requires consent, so do kissing, hooking up, and eventually sex. *Consent* is the word we use to describe when everybody involved enthusiastically, clearly, and verbally agrees that they are ready and want to move forward with any sexual experience . . . or with jumping out of a plane.

Let's say you really want to . . . ahem . . . go skydiving with someone. You're sure, and you know you're ready. Well, there are some rules about *skydiving* that you have to follow, just like you would if you jumped out of an airplane with someone. If you don't follow these rules, not only will you ruin your skydiving partner's experience, but you risk jail time, a lifetime of social consequences, and serious legal problems.

## TEN RULES FOR TANDEM SKYDIVING THAT ALSO APPLY TO HOOKING UP

**RULE 1:** Every time you want to jump out of an airplane with someone, you must ask if they also want to jump out of an airplane with you. It's easy. It goes like this: "Do you want to jump out of an airplane with me?" See? Wasn't that easy?

**RULE 2**: If someone says, "No, I don't want to jump out of an airplane with you," for any reason, then you don't get to jump out of an airplane with them.

**RULE 3**: You do not ever, *ever* get to push, pull, or force someone out of an airplane. You must ask them, "Are you ready to jump?" If they enthusiastically agree, "Omigod, yes! Let's do this!" that's when you get to jump out of an airplane with that person.

**RULE 4**: If someone says that they're "maybe" ready to jump out of an airplane, or they "aren't sure" if they're ready, then that means no, they are not ready to jump out of an airplane with you. "I don't know" means "no."

**RULE 5**: If someone agrees to go up in an airplane with you just to look around and see what it might be like to jump out of an airplane with you, you do not get to grab them, clip them to yourself, and jump out of the airplane with them. You still have to ask if they want to jump. And they have to enthusiastically agree.

**RULE 6**: Everybody is allowed to change their mind about skydiving at any time. If someone says they want to go skydiving with you, then they go up in an airplane with you and say, "I've changed my mind and don't want to go skydiving with you anymore," then you might be disappointed, but you don't get to jump from an airplane with them.

**RULE 7**: If someone agrees to go skydiving with you once, and you have a great time, it does not mean that you get to clip yourself to them whenever you want and make them go skydiving with you every day.

**RULE 8**: Just because other people in the past have enthusiastically agreed to jump out of an airplane with you, it does not mean that every future jumper automatically agrees. You must ask each person you want to jump out of an airplane with.

**RULE 9**: If someone is sleeping, you do not get to attach yourself and jump out of an airplane. Nobody likes waking up to skydiving. Ever.

**RULE 10**: If someone isn't sure about jumping out of a plane with you, you don't get to manipulate them to jump with you, you don't get to pressure them to jump, you don't get to threaten them until they jump, you don't get to intimidate them until they jump, and you don't get to give them drugs or alcohol until they jump. If you have a position of superiority or power over someone else, such as being their team captain, class president, or anything else, you do not get to dangle rewards like more game time or improved social status in order to get someone to go

skydiving with you. You also don't get to threaten punish-
ments like less game time or ruined social status.

Here's the thing: If you're already falling out of the sky and you
ask, "Is this okay with you?" you haven't given the other person an
actual choice. If you imply or say that you know better because
you're more experienced, or if you stoke fear over not jumping,
then you are taking away someone else's rightful choice. That's not
cool; that's toxic. Definitely also toxic is using name-calling, threats,
or your power to get them to jump when they're not ready. In fact,
there's a name for those things: it's called coercion. It's illegal.

To be super clear, let's drop the skydiving analogy and talk
about what you can say before hooking up with someone.

An easy and very appealing phrase is: "I'd really like to kiss you
right now. Would that be okay?"

For moving beyond kissing, you can ask, "Would you like it if I
_____ ?" Or you can ask, "Do you want to_____?" and then you fill
in the blank with a very clear description of what you'd like to do.

When the day comes that you're emotionally, mentally, and
physically mature enough to have sex, you absolutely—no possible
exceptions—must ask, out loud, if they are ready as well. You can
say, "I want to have sex with you. Are you ready for that?" If that
isn't something you can do, you are not ready to be sexual with
another person.

You're only ready if you have asked a question that requires a
very clear yes or no, *from the other person's perspective*.

Here are examples of less-than-great ways to go about this. If
you say, "I want to_____" or "I'd like to start _____, okay?" then you
aren't asking what the other person wants. You're just saying what

your desires are or what you're about to do. Think about it: if they say, "Okay," to either of those questions, then that person hasn't actually said that they also want what you're interested in. They've only said that they understand your desire.

When you're in a relationship and you've already been physical to any degree, you should still ask before getting physically intimate again by saying, "Are you in the mood for_____? I am."

Every time you're interested in being sexual, you need to ask. It's called consent, which is a heavy word, but in practice, and when done right, asking for it can be a really, really big turn-on.

At any stage of any relationship, if you hear a verbal "yes" in return to your question, then the next part of your mission is to be totally present. Physical connection—on any level—is a wildly real thing to share with another human. So be there. Be present for the person you're sharing that experience with. Care for them in a way that makes them feel cared for. And honor yourself, too, making sure that you are cared for and loved. Because you deserve that from the person who shares their body with you in any way.

# AND THAT'S A WRAP ON THE SEX STUFF

Wherever you're at on your journey with this stuff—dating, getting to know yourself sexually, making your choices about porn, thinking about sex, asking someone on a date, wanting to go further, looking for love, or still just confused—know this: You are exactly where you should be. You're good, man. It's totally cool to be where you're at with this stuff.

And mad props to ya! You got real here. We took it heavy. And talking about this stuff? Let me just say it's not a small thing. It says a lot about you, that you were willing to "go there." Thanks for being an awesome human and for awesomely honoring other humans! Now? Let's get you started on the final phase of your training!

# TRAINING PHASE III

## BATTLE TACTICS

Pit your every soul against the unknown
and seek stimulation in the comfort of the brave.
Experience cold, hunger, heat and thirst
and survive to see
another challenge
and another dawn.
Only then will you be at peace
with yourself
and be able to know and to say,
"I look down the farthest side of the mountain,
fulfilled and understanding all,
and truly content that
I lived a full life and one
that was my own choice."

—JAMES ELROY FLECKER, ENGLISH NOVELIST AND PLAYWRIGHT

# CHALLENGE 7: CARRY ANTIVENOM

Masculinity doesn't require that you be perfect,
only that you acknowledge your imperfections,
take responsibility, and clean your own mess up.

—JASYN JONES,
BLOGGER AND HOST OF *GEEK GAB* PODCAST

# LETHAL TOXINS EXPERT

People see you as the iconic definition of a man's man. "Double sun power!" the world said, quoting your Old Spice commercials (commercials that feature your shredded bare abs. In the *Expendables* franchise, you appear next to Sylvester Stallone, Jet Li, Jean-Claude Van Damme, Randy Couture, and Chuck Norris . . . and you tower over every one of them. And you've received no shortage of fan love and critical acclaim for your comedic macho role on *Brooklyn Nine-Nine*.

But today, in Washington, DC, it's not about what you've done in the past. Today you stand proud because of what you're about to do. *This is the purpose of my life,* you think as you slide a red pin through the lapel of your suit coat. *Today I am defending human rights.* The pin says RISE in white letters.

Today, there will be no acting. Today will be more like when you played defensive end and linebacker in the NFL, when you said "No way" to your opponents, play after play.

You look into your own eyes in the mirror. You're considered one of the best-dressed men in Hollywood. Today, your cuff links and freshly shaved head project the perfect balance of gentlemanly class and I-don't-take-crap-from-anyone. You nod to yourself, then exit the bathroom and walk through the hallways of the Capitol, past stone heads of several founding fathers. Your footfalls on the historic floor echo through the sunlit hallway. Rounding a turn, you find civil rights activist and Nobel Peace Prize nominee Amanda Nguyen. She's your Battle Crew today, and she's ready. You both are. Without speaking, the two of you lock step and head toward the chamber to fight the same war. To testify in front of a full chamber of United States senators.

The double doors are opened for you and you're shown to your chair, facing a panel of elected officials. Every seat is full. Cameras start rolling, and a court stenographer begins writing every word that's said.

You're here defending the law that Amanda and her organization, Rise, have drafted. It's your hope that your testimony will help this bill become a federal law governing all fifty states.

Amanda is invited to speak first. She explains, "On the day that I was raped, I never could have imagined that a greater injustice awaited me than the one I was already forced to endure." The senators give her the respect every human deserves: They listen. So do you.

Rape is being forced to have sex with someone. It's sex without consent and against your will. Rape is an assault that is physically, mentally, emotionally, and spiritually abusive to another human.

After her assault, Amanda wanted to press charges, but she had an internship with NASA lined up. And she still had to graduate from Harvard. She decided that she wasn't going to drop everything in her life to confront her assailant in a court of law, because legal battles over sexual assaults often take years and require expensive lawyers. She simply didn't have the resources. So she decided that instead of further derailing her life, she'd graduate and begin working at NASA.

During her NASA internship, something continued to weigh on Amanda. She kept thinking about how it was nearly impossible to secure her own rape kit—a collection of evidence of sexual assault—from the hospital where she was examined after her attack. In fact, after six months, her records would be destroyed unless she filled out tedious, hard-to-find, and retraumatizing forms.

One day, Amanda confided in her boss at NASA that she wanted to get a new law written and passed . . . but she was worried that if she pressed the pause button on her career, it would ruin her chances of becoming an astronaut. Amazingly—and really, think just how awesome his answer was—her boss told her with his full support and reassurance: "Space is still gonna be there."

That's what led Amanda to create Rise. It's the organization that brought you, worldwide macho man, to sit in front of these United States senators. You're here to do something about it. You're here to ensure that the Survivors' Bill of Rights gets passed.

Because you, too, were sexually assaulted.

Yes, you—massive, muscled, world-renowned comedic actor, former NFL linebacker—are the survivor of a sexual assault.

That's why you're in the halls of Congress today. You've been invited to introduce yourself and tell your story. Because when a

celebrity gets involved in a cause, people seem to listen harder. You're using the power of your celebrity to make lasting change for good. Because of your own life story, you know all too well how important this bill is.

When it's your turn, you say, "I believed, to my core, that as a man, I was more valuable in this world than women. [That] as a protector, and symbol of strength, I was more worthy, that women were beneath me." You go on: "As a man, I was taught my entire life that I must control the world. So I used power, influence, and control, to dominate every situation: from the football field to the film set, even in my own home with my wife and children. Then, in 2016, at a party with my wife, I was sexually assaulted by a successful Hollywood agent.

"The assault lasted only minutes, but what he was effectively telling me, while he held my genitals in his hand, was that he held the power. That he was in control."

The memory sears your brain. You explain that you couldn't believe what was happening . . . you were the biggest, baddest dude at the party. Then, suddenly, a high-level executive comes over and gropes you. You pushed him back, saying, "Stop! What are you doing?" Then, in front of your wife, he came back and did it again.

As you relive the trauma in front of the assembled senators, your shoulders tense. You explain how a toxic culture tried to humiliate and silence you because you spoke out against a powerful, well-connected man who abused his power.

Here's what happened next: the day after the attack, you went to the heads of the guy's company to report what happened. "What are you gonna do about it?" you demanded.

Their answer was: "You know, that's just the way it goes. . . ."

You felt devalued. You felt ashamed. You wondered if anyone would believe you. Beyond that, the agency was making you a lot of money. You thought, *This is the guy givin' me 20 million dollars, what am I going to do? Am I going to risk everything and call him out?*

You kept your mouth shut. For weeks. Weirdly, in that time, you thought a lot about your four-year-old self. Your very first memory in life was your father punching your mother in the face as hard he could. Abuse has been a familiar script in your life. For you, it's easy to think, *That's just the way it goes.*

Then, in the media, you heard about women sharing their stories of being assaulted by powerful people who refused to be held accountable. Those women gave you the courage to come forward publicly. You realized, *I devalue myself by saying that abuse is no big* deal. *That takes away my worth. That's minimizing. And nobody should be made to feel less than human.*

Without giving a heads-up to your costars or your wife, you did what you needed to do for you. You told the world the truth of your story.

After explaining on Twitter what had happened, you instantly experienced the cultural backlash that many survivors face. You were intimidated, you were shamed, you were threatened, you were mocked.

You deflected every one of these tactics, all designed to keep you silent about the assault.

That's the sequence of events that led you here, to this legislative hearing. "I'm not a small or insecure man," you tell the senators, fortifying your voice before concluding with, "This is how toxic masculinity permeates culture. . . . I was told over and over that this was not abuse. That this was just a joke. That this was just horseplay. But I choose to stand in solidarity with millions of other survivors. I know how hard it is to come forward. I know the shame associated with assault. It happened to me."

# TERRY CREWS: DEFENDING HUMAN RIGHTS

The True Warriors in the Rise organization and True Warriors Amanda Nguyen and Terry Crews (whose story this is) convinced Congress to unanimously pass the Sexual Assault & Survivors' Bill of Rights. The vote was 399–0 and it was signed into law by President Barack Obama.

Rise, Amanda, and Terry defended their tribe by succeeding at

Challenge 7: They stood up to toxic behaviors when they saw them. And they were brave enough to recognize the horrible effects of this toxic behavior and didn't stop until they got the right antivenom to the right people.

I put you in Terry's shoes so that you could see and experience this truth: abuse isn't about gender. It's not only "a girl problem." One in four girls is sexually assaulted before she turns eighteen—and one in seven boys will be sexually assaulted before the age of eighteen.

If that person is you, or you think it may be you, know this right now: You are loved. You are not alone. What happened to you is screwed up. It's *not* your fault. It's *not* right. You are not less of a man. You have absolutely nothing to be ashamed of. You were abused and taken advantage of.

No matter your story, you need to know that sexual assault is not the only kind of abuse that counts as abuse. Emotional violence affects men as well. Same goes for mental violence, verbal violence, and spiritual violence. In my experience, talking about it with a trusted adult (someone who is not involved with what happened in any way) is not only suggested, but it's required.

Why's that? It's because with all types of abuse, there is a much greater risk of post-traumatic stress disorder, depression, alcoholism, drug abuse, suicidal thoughts and attempts, relationship problems, and underachievement in school and at work. If we warriors are going to protect ourselves and our tribes, then we have to acknowledge that not only is this very real for men and women alike, but it comes with long-term consequences. It doesn't have to, though. We can face this problem head-on.

This challenge is about shutting down every kind of toxic mistreatment of any person, no matter who it's from or toward. This could be the challenge that requires the most courage to succeed at, because it's incredibly hard for guys to feel accepted and talk about it. Here's proof: men with documented histories of sexual abuse (by social service agencies) are four times less likely than women to even admit to themselves that they've been abused, let alone seek help or talk about what happened with someone else.

If you're someone thinking, *Oh, that'll never affect me* or *This isn't important to guys,* let me tell ya . . . if you remain oblivious to how this affects everyone, you might as well start running barefoot and naked through a poison oak forest full of scorpions and stinging nettles. You're gonna end up getting stung by something. I can guarantee you that, in your life, you will encounter toxic people. And while you may not have attacked someone, we're all a part of the culture. Me and you both. That's why . . .

**Challenge 7 is to know how to identify the symptoms of having toxic humans in your life. You will succeed at this challenge by knowing the evidence to look for and then being ready to apply the antivenom when it's needed.**

You're going to get everything you need right here. But brace yourself. This stuff is heavy. You'll need to bring your A game.

# POISON VS. VENOM

Snakes kill 90,000 people each year and disable tens, maybe hundreds, of thousands more. But did you know that some are poisonous while others are venomous?

If you're like me, you had no idea there was a difference. But it's true. Poisonous and venomous creatures are not the same:

**Poisonous creatures** use their toxins *to defend* themselves from predators.

**Venomous creatures** use their toxins *to attack* their prey.

Poisonous creatures are misunderstood. They are boundary-setters, saying, "If you attack me, I will feel scared of being eaten. I will have to poison you. I don't want to poison you, but I will if I have to. I hope we can go back to being friends." Poisonous frogs and plants and urchins totally have every right to defend themselves!

In the same way, if you've hurt someone's feelings and it was a genuine accident, that just means you're human.

But venomous creatures? They go on the prowl. They hunt, intentionally trying to inject toxins into their prey.

If you notice you've hurt someone and start to wonder if you're the venomous one, all you have to do is look at what your original intent was before things got all weird. We're allowed to have poisonous edges to our personalities. We're allowed to defend ourselves. But we are not allowed to be *venomous*. *Venomous* implies bad intent—the purpose is to hurt someone.

That might have you asking . . . how can I know if there's a venomous human in my life? And, maybe more important, how do I find the antivenom?

# FOUR SIGNS THAT TOXIC PEOPLE ARE IN YOUR LIFE

Let's say you're walking down the street and suddenly a death-stalker scorpion stabs you in your pinky toe. But here's the thing: You never saw the ugly little critter. Still, your body would automatically react to the venom, right? You didn't have to see it happen to know you're being affected by the venom. How? Because you'll experience the list of symptoms that the scorpion's venom causes in a person.

With the venom of a deathstalker scorpion in your blood, your muscles will shake uncontrollably; then you'll start sweating and barfing everywhere. Your belly will hurt like you ate four-month-old tuna that was left out in the sun, and while your lungs are filling with fluid, your digestive tract will rapidly eject anything you've eaten over the past three days.

Fun, right?

You don't need to know the specific strategies that abusers use. You don't even need to know who an abusive person is. If you start experiencing the symptoms of being around a toxic human—you gotta treat it like a deathstalker scorpion sting! And you gotta get the antivenom in order to heal.

Toxic humans' actions bring about symptoms that are a little less obvious than toxic creatures'. And that's exactly what makes 'em so dangerous.

1. **You feel unreasonable tension.** When you're around a toxic person, you might frequently feel you are walking on eggshells, or dreading that you could do something wrong at any moment. You may find that you frequently have to explain your actions, apologize, or defend yourself—when you didn't even think that you did something wrong.

2. **You've changed for the worse.** Your thoughts and emotions have turned negative. You might feel completely sucked dry of joy and energy. Perhaps most telling is if you feel "less than" you were before a relationship started—*in any way.* You feel less confident, less secure, less intelligent,

less sane, less trusting, less attractive . . . if you feel less *any-thing*, something is toxic in your life.

3. **You've been silenced about something.** If you're asked to keep "a secret" about something that made you uncomfortable when it happened . . . or something that still makes you uncomfortable . . . or even if it feels like you want to talk about something, but it's not really safe to—that's silencing. Abusers need their victims to be unaware—or silent—in order to continue their abuse and keep getting away with it. In fact, they depend on it. That's toxic.

4. **You are avoiding . . . *anything*.** You find yourself spending less and less quality time with friends, family, your Battle Crew, or your tribe. Maybe you're spending no time with them at all. Perhaps you're avoiding the people, places, and activities that remind you of something that happened.

# HOW TO APPLY THE ANTIVENOM

If any one of those symptoms matches what you're dealing with right now, you need to apply the antivenom.

You know how Spider-Man got bitten by a radioactive spider to develop his superhuman strength and spider senses? Well, there is a real-life phenomenon by which humans can actually gain superhuman strength and detection skills if they're "bitten" by toxic humans.

Gaining superpowers from toxins is not just for comic books! If you've been injected with toxins, it's possible to come back *better than ever before.*

Here's the deal: The antivenom applies for *everyone.* Are you someone who's hearing about abuse for the first time? If you've been abused, if you are supporting someone else who's in an abusive situation, or even if you notice some abusive tendencies in yourself . . . the antivenom will still work.

## STEP 1: ADMIT TO THE SYMPTOMS

You've got to admit that the venom is affecting you and—whether you know how it happened or not—acknowledge what's happened. You must trust your intuition, your logic, and your body. When you see any of the four symptoms: unreasonable tension, a change for the worse, silencing, or avoidance . . . admit to it. Be real. Be honest with yourself. Then proceed to step 2.

## STEP 2: FIND THE PERSON WITH THE CORRECT ANTIVENOM

Next, you've got to find the person who has the specific kind of antivenom for the specific strain of toxin you're dealing with.

Aka you need a professionally qualified adult who will get in the trenches with you. Did you know that there are people whose only job is to help teenagers who have been affected by toxins? It's true! Ask the adult you trust most to help you find the right person.

Fortunately, for every kind of human toxic abuse that exists, we have discovered the antivenom. If you don't know who to speak to, the resources in the back of this book will get you started on your search for the right person. Do not stop searching until you've found someone you trust and who can help you. Step 2 is to find that person. Trust me, they're out there. They're ready to help you. And they *can* help make the pain and confusion go away. But it's up to you to have the courage to keep looking until you find the person with the correct antivenom for you.

## STEP 3: USE YOUR FIRE

Remember Amanda Nguyen? The woman who founded Rise? She gave an amazing speech where she told the audience, "After my rape, I felt despair. But I also felt fire." She used that fire to rewrite the law. After sharing what her organization does, she said, "That is what I did with my fire. What will you do with yours?"

After you've acknowledged the reality of your situation and found the right healer, you can now focus on healing, and maybe even helping others.

From here, you'll hopefully improve your boundary-setting skills. Specifically by choosing to leave the toxic relationship (or by getting great at keeping that person far, far away). Overall, it's easier and keeps your sanity intact when you simply extract the person from your life like they're a rotten tooth. It may be painful, but being assertive is less painful than dealing with abuse.

The second way to improve is to fine-tune your senses! If you feel unreasonable tension when someone is around you (and it's not the same kind of tension as "I'm in trouble for not finishing my homework"), then don't spend time with that person! Same thing applies if you notice that there's more drama in your group only when one specific person is around.

No matter what, you can improve by taking really good care of yourself. Rest is how we grow. So rest. Rest a lot. Eat healthy foods.

Exercise gently. Do the things you love to do. And make a dedicated effort to spend extra time with people who love you. If you're a friend supporting someone who's been victimized, get great at listening and understanding. Remind them, by your words and by your actions, that there's nothing wrong with them. Trust me . . . it will be ridiculously healing for them.

# FOR BEING THAT BRAVE

Terry Crews said in an interview that there still exists a little four-year-old boy inside him and that, when he was groped as an adult, that four-year-old part of him also "got molested. And that little boy is sitting in me thinking 'Who's going to fight for me?'"

I believe that each of us still has a four-year-old self deep in our heart. This little child is where the purest parts of us are—and is also where our deepest insecurities lie. Every guy and every girl has a four-year-old in their heart who needs protection.

If you trash-talk, laugh, and join in the name-calling at someone else's expense . . . if you shove, punch, intimidate, make fun of someone for their sexuality, their race . . . if you assault someone verbally, emotionally, physically, or in any other way . . . you are doing those things to that person's inner four-year-old. That's toxic. It's abusive. Don't be that person.

Terry says that "No man, woman, or child should ever put up with being treated as less than a human being. Never. Not ever." That kid in you, and the kid at the heart of everyone in your tribe, deserves to be cared for, looked after, and made to feel safe.

Right before Amanda and Terry shared their stories, Senator

Chuck Grassley told them, "This may be difficult, but thank you for being that brave."

That's the same reaction you can hope to receive when you confront toxins in your life: It'll be seen as incredibly brave. Part of your job, Warrior, is to eliminate toxins from the world when you encounter them.

If you're brave enough to admit to what's up, speak up to the right person, and grow by the fire, you can leave the world better than you found it.

Amanda said, "There's a long tradition of people taking their painful living truths and channeling that into justice." Step up and become one of those people she's talking about. Channel your truth into justice and carry the antivenom with you wherever you go.

# TRAINING GROUNDS:
## CARRY ANTIVENOM

### KNOW IT

Boys don't know how to deal with toxic people or don't even recognize that they exist. Warriors know how to deal with emotional, verbal, physical, sexual, or spiritual violence.

### ACT ON IT

☐ Can you repeat the four symptoms of Toxic Humans on pages 199–200? Does even a single symptom describe what you're experiencing? Be authentic and truthful with yourself. If the answer is yes, that's all you need to know, and it's time to seek out the antivenom.

☐ Commit to having the courage to speak up to the right person when you notice the effects of the toxins anywhere in your life.

☐ Decide right now that when you encounter venomous humans, you'll use the poison to grow as a person.

# CHALLENGE 8:
# CHOOSE YOUR BATTLEGROUND

Some people believe holding on and hanging
in there are signs of great strength. However,
there are times when it takes much more strength
to know when to let go and then do it.

## —ANN LANDERS,
### ADVICE COLUMNIST WHO HAD 90 MILLION READERS

# THE NOBLEST PIRATE

The red-and-orange light of sunrise spreads over the sea, illuminating the warship you've just stolen from the Charleston harbor. The paddle wheels on either side of the boat spray a continuous, steady mist on your crew while they propel you east toward the rising sun. As you make progress, the cool, wet air is beginning to smell less like the marshes and harbors of South Carolina's waterways and more like the Atlantic Ocean's salty breezes. Today is the first day of your life as a free man. And the first day of your life as a pirate.

The thirty-foot-wide deck of your steamboat—which, as of last night, belonged to the Confederate Navy—is loaded down with thousands of pounds of artillery and explosives. You and your crew are ready to fire at any bigot on a boat who tries to stop you on your path to freedom.

You review your mental list of the stolen weapons that are sitting on the deck of your ship.

- One 32-pound pivot gun, mounted to the bow. Medium-range ship sinker.
- One 24-pound Howitzer, 8-inch barrel, stern mounted. Short-range assault weapon.
- Four standard cannons, two for starboard defenses and two for port defenses.
- One banded 42-pound rifled gun (still dented from its battle at Fort Sumter, where the Civil War began one year ago).
- Two columbiad gun carriages, 8- and 10-inch barrels.
- 200 pounds of additional ammunition and gunpowder.

Escaping the South during the Civil War with a toddler, a new-born, your wife, and several of your friends and their families, was widely considered an impossible task. In this slave nation of the Confederate South, traveling north by foot with so many loved ones was a wild thought—your plan of escape had to be another approach entirely, something that had never been done. It had to be something that was so over-the-top courageous, nobody would ever suspect you would think of it. Something that, once the Confederates figured out what had happened, they'd still never believe because of the sheer backbone and audacity of it.

Now that the deed is done, you've become a pirate. A war criminal. A captain, traitor, leader. And soon, you'll undoubtedly have a bounty on your head. You've asked for none of these labels. The only descriptor you've ever wanted is "free man."

Yet one final step remains in your quest for freedom. If you succeed, you, your family, and your friends will finally be free. But if you fail? You will all be dead.

The CSS *Planter* is a Confederate States ship. The 147-foot-long steamboat was converted into a warship at the start of the war. You were indentured as its crew member, so you know every detail. Stealing it went off without a hitch. Your escape window began to form when the former captain, Charles J. Relyea, started taking the white crew members ashore several days a week. They'd leave you and the other slaves aboard the CSS *Planter* without locks of any kind, never thinking you'd be able to escape the harbor by foot. They also doubted, based solely on the color of your skin, that you'd have the skills to pilot the ship out of the harbor. Fortunately for your escape, racism and stupidity are very close cousins.

During those evenings alone, your crew hatched the plan. When you heard that the Union had created a blockade at the mouth of the harbor, cutting off the South's food supplies, you realized that the finish line had come to you. Sailing solo, hundreds of miles to the safety of the North, would have surely resulted in being hunted down. But now? You only had to make it out of the harbor and you'd join the Union and the largest concentration of warships on the planet. With any luck, they'd even escort you to New York or Boston or Philadelphia!

Last night, after darkness had descended, you and your crew were finally ready to move. After Relyea left, you put on his uniform. Wearing his long Confederate naval jacket and his military-issue captain's hat, you paced the deck with his exact gait. You couldn't believe you were doing it. You piled wood onto the engine's fire, causing the boiler to create steam; then you climbed the staircase up to the highest deck on the ship, where your body cut a dark figure against the giant white cloud from the smokestack. From that height, you spotted the shipyard's night patrol, just as you expected. They also saw you. You were dressed like Relyea, perfectly imitating his gestures, so everything looked like business as usual. The steam engine was pressurized, the waterwheels started turning, and the CSS *Planter* pushed off.

You even had the guts to wave goodbye to the guards. The Confederate Navy waved back *See ya!* as you stole their warship.

It's 1862, so explosive, ship-sinking mines are anchored across the floor of Charleston's harbor. It's literally an underwater minefield, making it impossible to navigate without precise knowledge of the placement of the bombs. Fortunately, when you were a slave, you laid many of the mines, so you also know how to avoid them.

In the dark, you motored to an agreed-on meeting spot, stopping to pick up your family and friends. Aboard your ship with you are seven men, five women, and three children—all of them run-aways, a crime punishable by death. Your crew has agreed that, if caught, you will scuttle the ship. *We will burn it in the water as our last act of freedom. If blowing it up fails, we will jump overboard. Better to die free than hang by their hands.*

You then headed east, where five heavily armed naval check-points awaited you. At each checkpoint, you paced the deck, mim-icking the captain. You ordered the ship's steam whistle to be sounded in the correct "password" at each stop—two long blasts followed by one short—and you were allowed to continue on your way out to sea. Belowdecks, your newborn baby boy slept silently. You were so grateful that he didn't cry at the horns. If he had, you and all of your passengers would surely be dead by now.

The final checkpoint was Fort Sumter. After you supplied the password, the commander shouted across the waters, "Give those Yankee bastards hell!" You yelled back, "Aye aye, sir!" and then busted up laughing as you turned toward the Union blockade.

Now the final part of your escape plan to freedom is happen-ing. The *Planter* is still in danger of being blasted out of the water. Not by your own hands, and not by the Confederates. It's suddenly the Union Navy whose cannons are trained directly on you, your crew, and the *Planter*.

The sun is rising behind the Union's warships, making their long black shadows stretch across the waters. Despite the intimidating sight, you take a moment to appreciate the first sunrise you've ever seen as a free man. But if those ships don't realize you're not their enemy, it'll be your last.

To finally be free *and* safe, you need the Union commander to understand exactly what's just happened: Sixteen slaves from

South Carolina—a Southern state—just stole a Confederate Navy warship, the CSS *Planter,* on this 386th day of the United States Civil War, May 13, 1862. If the commander doesn't see who is aboard the enemy warship that's charging straight at his naval blockade, he will order his men to fire, and your family's path to freedom will come to a swift end.

"Full steam ahead!" you cry to your crew. The paddle wheels of your lonely steamboat grip hard against the salt water and barrel you at full speed toward the Union Navy's greatest concentration of power.

"And lower that flag already!" you yell. The Confederate flag slides down the pole, and your men begin to hoot and holler. You swear it will never fly on this vessel again. This ship doesn't stand for what that racist cloth represents.

"All hands on deck!" Women and children begin to emerge from below and spread out among the cannons. Everyone starts waving and shouting, as if for a rescue.

"Remove your hats and coats!" you order the families. You need the Navy to see that nobody on board has white skin.

Despite your efforts, your worst fears are coming true. The Union ships are moving into defensive positions. *They think we're a Rebel ramming ship on a sacrificial collision course.*

The USS *Onward* raises its cannons into attack position. *They're gonna blow us out of the water!*

Excitement turns to cold fear, and your crew starts saying good-bye to their families.

The glow of a fire shines through the *Onward*'s port-side hatch. The flame is from the artilleryman's torch. He's preparing to ignite the gunpowder! That flickering dot of red light means that cannon No. 3 is trained directly on your ship, loaded, and ready to fire.

Aboard the *Planter*, whoever isn't crying is holding their breath. What happens next will only be one of two things: Cannon fire. Or freedom.

*Come on . . . come on . . . figure it out!*

Your eyes scan the shadows of the ships and you spot the commander's silhouette. You know it's him because his arm is raised. If he lowers that arm, all sixteen of you will be dead.

To your surprise, your wife's voice fills the air: "Fly the surrender flag!" she cries with an authority that any captain would envy.

Hannah, always thinking, has brought up a white bedsheet from belowdecks! As it's hoisted up the mast, she tells you that she snatched it from the hotel where she worked before meeting you at the rendezvous point. The knots of the flag line smack into the top of the flagpole, and the white "surrender" sheet billows open.

All these souls, under your leadership, await their fate, wondering, *Will this be the end of our lives or the start of whatever we want to make of ourselves?*

It's faint.

But unmistakable.

*A voice.*

You make out the words floating over the ocean's humid air: "Hold your fire! White flag! No white men on board! White flag!"

"They figured it out!" you holler to your crew.

After a pause, your wife cheers, and the newly freed passengers of the CSS *Planter* erupt in celebration. Your friends start dancing amid the cannons. The children are giggling. Some begin singing hymns, while others are "muttering maledictions" back in the direction of Fort Sumter. (Just so there's no confusion: "muttering maledictions" is 1800s talk for cursing at the racists hiding in the fort.)

You? You're watching the celebration with awe and joy, but what's happening hasn't even begun to sink in. Today is the day you demanded and fought for your family's rightful freedom—indeed, independence should have been theirs, and yours, all along.

# ROBERT SMALLS: ESCAPE ARTIST

This is the real-life story of True Warrior Robert Smalls. I'm not kidding when say I wonder if he was born with a backbone made of reinforced titanium.

I get chills—and teary eyed—every time I think about the moment those passengers realized they were safe and began shouting and dancing.

And, yes, you're justified in thinking: *How does a privileged white male from twenty-first-century America possibly identify with the plight of a biracial Civil War–era former slave who had to risk life and limb for his family to be free?*

That is a great question.

My answer? It's what Robert Smalls did with his life that breathes life into me. That man makes me want to be a better human. His story inspires me to no end. It makes me want to honor his legacy through what I do in my world, today.

Every time I read about it, his story becomes even more

amazing, especially when you consider his upbringing. Robert Smalls was born in a shack. His white slave-owner father most likely raped his mother, resulting in her pregnancy. Being biracial, Smalls had a hard time feeling accepted by either race. When he turned ten, his mother took him to see the public whipping post and to witness slave auctions, just to be sure that young Robert understood the reality of their world. Understanding just how demoralizing, frightening, and infuriating that must have been is impossible for many of us in today's world.

When he became old enough to take shipyard jobs, Robert was allowed to keep only 12.5 percent of his salary—one dollar per week. The other seven dollars went to his slave master (and father).

In his early twenties, he met and married his wife, Hannah. They had a baby girl, and Robert was told that the "purchase price" of his family's freedom was $800. When he heard the number, he immediately began saving. Otherwise he, his daughter, or Hannah could be sold, never to see one another again. Which was common. Indeed, everything related to and surrounding slavery is a dark stain on America's history.

When Smalls and Hannah had their second child and were told the purchase price would go up, he decided enough was enough. He'd do whatever it took to escape.

After linking up with the other ships, Smalls surrendered the CSS *Planter* and its artillery to the Union. His crew also delivered maps of underwater mines, intel on army positions, and perhaps most important, the communication codebook containing the keys to crossing every Confederate naval checkpoint.

But even more amazing? His heist of a warship isn't what makes Robert Smalls a True Warrior. This is just one of the many times

Smalls did something jaw-droppingly inspiring and unbelievable.

When Smalls and his crew surrendered the *Planter,* he was given a substantial reward. But Robert didn't just take the money and call it good.

Instead, he kept fighting. Then, win or lose, he picked the next battle. And kept fighting. Decade after decade, for the rest of his life, he continued to choose the most pressing, most important battle in front of him and tackle injustice after injustice—right up to the day he died. *That* is what makes him one of the most incredible heroes of the Civil War and, in my opinion, world history.

After relocating to the North, he learned that black people weren't actually allowed to fight in the Union Army's military. You know who changed that? Robert Smalls.

The story goes: A Northern officer named David Hunter had gone rogue. Illegally, he trained close to 50,000 soldiers, all of them former slaves who were ready to fight for the North. But they weren't allowed to because of the color of their skin. So there was this massive trained army of former slaves, hiding out on an island, ready to go to war. When Smalls heard about this, he had already returned to the South. What did he do? He got on a horse and trotted a casual 1,065 miles across America—as a runaway slave, during the Civil War, with a giant bounty on his head—to Washington, DC, to talk some sense into the secretary of war.

But before he could meet the guy, Smalls got interrupted . . . by none other than President Abraham Lincoln. Lincoln, after hearing about the boat heist, wanted to meet Smalls and invited him to the White House. Lincoln asked him. "Why did you do what you did?" Smalls answered with one word: "Freedom."

Then, with Lincoln's blessing, Smalls lobbied the secretary of war with such conviction that eventually 179,000 African American soldiers enlisted in the Union Army and another 19,000 in the Navy. Smalls even personally recruited 5,000 soldiers!

Most historians will tell you that the North would not have won the Civil War had it not been for African American forces. Every one of those American heroes fought as a direct result of the efforts of True Warrior Robert Smalls. Historians will also tell you that Lincoln's meeting with Smalls strongly influenced Lincoln to clearly define the purpose of the Civil War to be about that one word: freedom. And that was why, in his 1863 Gettysburg Address, he said that America "shall have a new birth of freedom." Smalls impressed and influenced Lincoln *that much*.

Did Smalls stop there? He did not. He fought in at least eighteen major battles or armed conflicts against Southern troops. At one point, he even got out of a boat and pushed it up a river while simultaneously being shot at by Confederates.

And after the Civil War ended, did he stop? He did not. Back then, it was illegal for black people in many American states to read and write. Smalls decided to change that. But because he was biracial, he couldn't stand the idea of an all-black or all-white school. So he founded the first-ever compulsory public school in the United States, making it legal for any child to enroll, regardless of skin color. In many ways, Smalls was the father of the United States' public school system.

He started a newspaper in Beaufort, South Carolina.

He became one of the first elected African American congressmen, first in the House of Representatives and then the Senate.

On and on goes his list of incredible accomplishments.

Robert Smalls, with each new era of his life, just kept moving forward, tackling each new injustice he saw, bringing all of the first seven True Warrior traits to each new trial he faced. That's how Smalls succeeded at Challenge 8, the ultimate True Warrior challenge.

**Challenge 8 is to choose your battleground. That means to boldly go forward, making your life a masterpiece, as you stay true to yourself and tackle injustice after injustice. You will know you've succeeded at this challenge when you choose the next battleground for yourself and commit to bringing what you've learned as a Warrior to your next fight.**

That's where this challenge comes from. And, you know me by now, so do I even need to explain that we're diving right in?

# ABOUT YOUR PAST . . .

Straight up: It is literally impossible for me, as a white guy in modern America, to make any assumptions about Smalls's state of mind. Not only are historical records from that time period a little lacking, but more important? It would be a Grand Canyon–sized leap for me to claim to understand what was going on in a former slave's mind. What I know for sure is that he displayed all the Warrior traits. And he spent his life using those traits to fight battles of enormous importance. All the research I've done on him tells me that he had these traits in spades—and then some.

Out of respect for Smalls's life and his story—which, as I said, goes beyond my identification—I am going to diverge from the usual setup here and talk from my own life experience. Here's what I've learned about what he did so well: choosing battles of enormous importance.

# STARTING FRESH

For me, I've found it helps immensely to start fresh when I take on new life projects. It's how I get the clarity to decide what the right next step is.

One way to do that? Let go.

Like, you can't very well enjoy high school if you keep wishing you're in the fourth grade, right? And I mean, if you get married one day, you'll let go of being single. If you have children, you will give up a lot of things. And when you die, you'll give up your life.

All our most significant moments in life require that we give something up or let something go, don't they? Those are easy examples . . . but it can get much harder.

Perhaps you once had a great friendship or relationship, but it's no longer the same and it's time to let it fade. Maybe there's a painful memory that you need to release, like a betrayal or a traumatic event. It could be letting go of an old identity, like when you moved cities or changed sports teams, or letting go of caring what other people think about who you choose to love. Maybe it's letting go of boyhood and deciding to be a man.

You don't need to let go of *everything*. Just what isn't working anymore.

Ask yourself: What have you grown out of? What is no longer right for you?

Identifying what we need to let go of is rarely the hard part. Deep down, we know what we should move on from. The *real* challenge is being strong enough to release our grip. Because, often, the most badass thing we can do is to let go.

Just in case you need some inspiration for where to start, these have been the most useful things I've let go of in my own Warrior journey:

## EXPECTATIONS

Quit worrying about becoming the fake person you think other people want you to be. Nobody has the power to make anyone happy but themselves. That means you gotta do what makes you happy and be the person you are happy with being. You're not here to please other people. Plus you'll definitely never rock anybody's world by desperately trying to be somebody you're not. Let go of the need to change who you are for the sake of fitting in or making other people comfortable. Let go of your need to care so much about upsetting people. Let go of trying to be who you imagine other people might want you to be, and instead be you. Besides, if people don't accept you for you, they aren't your people anyway. Anyone who truly loves you will want you to be true to yourself first and foremost.

## EXCUSES

What are you holding yourself back from? Usually, we make excuses when we're too scared to ask for what we really want. We take the easy way out by making up some bogus reason for not fighting for or asking for the things we know will be good for us.

Instead, we take the scaredy-cat route by telling ourselves no before we even give someone else the option to say yes. Cut that crap out and let go of the excuses you're telling yourself for . . .

- Why you won't apply to the college of your dreams.
- Why you won't ask that special person out on a date.
- Why you won't say you're sorry.

- Why you won't run for a leadership position.
- Why you're not talking to a therapist on a regular basis.
- Why you won't fight the biggest social injustice that pisses you off.

You know what your excuses are. You don't need them anymore, and they aren't helping. Let 'em go!

## RELATIONSHIPS

There are people who were once in your life for a reason. And now they aren't. Honestly, the why of it doesn't really matter. End of the day, everyone else is also trying to make their life a masterpiece. This means, keepin' the metaphor going, that other people have the right to choose to work with different artists and on different canvases when they make the artistic decision to do so . . . whether you agree with it or not. Sometimes you're meant to share the same paintbrushes, and sometimes you aren't.

Letting go doesn't mean you stop caring, but it does mean you stop trying to force others to. As author Steve Maraboli says: "Letting go means to come to the realization that some people are a part of your history, but not a part of your destiny."

## GRUDGES

People mess up and make mistakes. Sorry, kid, but you're gonna get hurt out there.

Forgiving someone who has hurt you is possibly the greatest expression of letting go. It's been said that "To forgive is to set a prisoner free."

Only catch? The prisoner isn't the other person. It's you.

"Forgiveness ain't about all of a sudden saying 'nothing happened,'" says Terry Crews. "Forgiveness is for me. Forgiveness is so I can move on. Forgiveness is so I can wipe my hands and go to the next step.

"But accountability is different. Accountability says, 'Hey, man, I don't trust you. And you're going to stay way over here. I forgive you, but I also know who you are. You understand where I'm at. I understand where you're at. And now we can be at peace.'"

His point is that forgiveness isn't about giving someone else a hall pass. It's about giving yourself what you deserve. You deserve to be freed from the hurt and injury that was done to you. Enforce your boundaries and the consequences for crossing them, but also let go and forgive. That's the only way to free ourselves of the energy we'd otherwise spend on holding a grudge. And if you're fortunate enough to receive someone else's forgiveness for your own wrong, hold on to that.

## ONE DAY, EVERYTHING

One day, you will have to let go of everything. Everything you've created, everything you've studied, everything you've built, everyone you've met. One day, it will all be gone. And you'll be gone, too. There are a lot of ideas about what happens when we die, but pretty much everybody agrees on this: we all will die someday. I know that sounds miserable to think about . . . but in my experience, accepting the fact that it's all a temporary gift is the best possible way to make your time on Earth become incredibly worthwhile. This is not a dress rehearsal. This is your life, right now.

No matter where you think we came from or what will happen next, the fact that this life is temporary is not sad. I think that's exactly what makes being alive so amazing. This world is a beautiful place, and staying anchored to something when it's time to let go is no way to live. My friend, it's time to set sail.

So why are you wasting your time holding on to what you know you shouldn't? Let it go. That's really the only way to go forward. It's the only way to shape your life into a masterpiece.

# YOUR PASSION AND PURPOSE

When you open up all that new space in your life, it'll be like clearing off a countertop to set down something new.

But if you let something go, what are you supposed to put in its place? What battles should you fight?

That's entirely up to you. The only person who can define your King of Beasts is the person whose eyeballs are reading this sentence.

I know, not very helpful, right?

But luckily, I have a solid starting place for you: You've got to have a purpose. You need to be working *toward something*.

Boys consume while men produce. You, as a boy, cost money. You eat food. You need school supplies and clothes. You need housing.

No need to feel guilty. That's where you are in life, and it's fine. So before you freak out and sign an apartment lease, build your independence slowly.

Ask your family for help with the specifics, but begin asking how you can start to produce. "How can I learn to provide?" is an awesome question to ask.

Maybe you already have a job, or you do chores to earn an allowance. Either way, you can go small at first and simply make some suggestions: Offer to make dinner once a week. Offer to pack your own lunches or to help pay for your sneakers. Start socking money away, slowly, for something you want. Make your bed every morning as a sign of respect for yourself.

Ask a parent: "What do you need from me in order for your life to be just a little bit easier?"

That's a super manly moment, not kidding. A lot of grown adults can't ask that question of each other.

One last thing about producing and having purpose: When you start thinking about what you're going to do for the rest of your life, don't get bogged down by this idea that you have to be paid for your passion.

If you can figure out how to get paid for doing what you love, that's awesome. But it's also totally legit to get paid for something that's not your life's purpose. Your passion project does not need to be something that you get paid for.

Let me say that differently: You can gladly get paid for something that isn't your top-priority passion in life. You can proudly wait tables. You can proudly work as an intern. You can proudly scrub floors. You can proudly work at a retail counter or sell something you aren't over-the-moon excited about.

Every one of those jobs made my life richer, figuratively *and* literally, by paying the bills. I've done *all* those things while making very little money with my passion projects (like climbing the world's tallest mountains, learning to kitesurf, writing my first book, traveling the world, and volunteering).

What I'm saying is this: When you're starting out, don't ever think that a job is beneath you. And don't make the mistake of feeling guilty if you're not turning your life's greatest passion into an ATM. *You don't have to!*

But no matter what, you should definitely have both a passion and a purpose. What that looks like for you is going to be up to your own unique design.

# CHARACTER DESIGN

Talking about passion and purpose is kind of a big-picture discussion. But what about from hour to hour and minute to minute? Who should you be in the moment?

When I asked for dating advice in high school, I heard people say, "Just be confident! Be yourself!"

I was like, "Okay, great . . . *who's that?*"

(And, side note, anybody else feel like "just be yourself" is the worst dating tip in the world?)

Better, here's something you can use to figure out who you are, right now. This doesn't just work for dating. It works for everything.

Have you ever played an RPG video game where you have to select character attributes? Like, you get to select a value for strength, stamina, speed, hit points, stuff like that?

Okay, so, character design in real life is doing that same thing . . . with yourself. There are only five toggle switches. And just like with any toggle, when you set it for one thing, it usually turns off the other.

But the settings aren't permanent! In fact, at any minute in life, you can come back to this page and choose to reset any of the toggles again, selecting the kind of character you're gonna play the game of life with. These can change multiple times per day, or they may stay the same for years. It's really up to you and the filters you want to apply to your artwork. You with me?

How do you know which toggle setting to choose? Well, you ask what your core, your true self, what the person holding this book, right now, needs. "What character traits would make the game of life really freaking awesome right now?"

Then you calibrate the settings to match what you need. Nobody's version is right or wrong—it's just about how each artist creates their masterpiece. Here are the five toggles to choose within:

## STRENGTH OR WARMTH?

You must be wise enough to know when to be tough and when to be tender. Just look at Smalls. One moment he's cuddling his baby. The next he's loading a cannon or pushing steamships upriver. Which is right for you in this moment?

## REST OR ACTION?

Warriors know when to produce and when to rest. Most guys either work their tails off or kick back and play a little too much. Guys are rarely good at doing both. Change that. Get off the hamster wheel, man. Just stop already. Or get on it, if it's time. Take the rest that you need to recover and come back from injury. Or illness. Or heartache. Or mourning. Rest is a part of taking action. And we need action to earn our rest. Make both a part of your life.

## EXCLUDE OR UNITE?

You've got to be wise enough to know when to unite and when to exclude. Shackleton had a rule: If one man needed tea, everyone got tea. He unified his men. Yet two of his men tried to turn against him in mutiny. Later, Shackleton excluded those two from being awarded medals by the English government. Be as wise as Shackleton, having the timing and courage to both exclude and unite.

## COMPETE OR PEACEKEEP?

Competition makes your body produce testosterone. Plain and simple, that's what happens. Men physically need competition. So don't be shy about letting your competitive edge go free. But when you do, never shame your opponent. Be assertive, but not aggressive. Stand your ground when you're challenged. Stand up for others. Never go beyond what somebody else can handle. By competing well, when the time comes to keep the peace, you will have stronger ground to stand on so that you can get the job done. Don't forget that peacekeeper Warriors are the most heroic in all of human history.

## RELATIONSHIP OR INDEPENDENCE?

Sometimes being in a relationship is the manly move. Life is often more fun when you're doing your thing with someone you love. But then again, sometimes flying solo is the manly move. In fact, it's often when we're independent that we learn to truly love ourselves. But please, don't fall into this trap of thinking that you have to love every aspect of yourself before you can seek out meaningful relationships. After all, it's often *through* relationships—with others who love us—that we understand we are lovable and learn to love ourselves.

# YOU: BATTLEGROUND MASTER

But I can't end a chapter that started with Robert Smalls with a bunch of stuff about me. I have to end it with him, his legacy, and everything he stood for. His story is the culmination of all the challenges that have come before. He, like all the men we've met, is what every one of us could aspire to be. And if you become a master at choosing your battlegrounds wisely, like he did, you will become that man.

I've given you my best advice for making that happen, but now? It's up to you.

# TRAINING GROUNDS:
## CHOOSE YOUR BATTLEGROUND

### KNOW IT

Boys hold on to the past and are afraid to move forward. A True Warrior lets go, forgives, and boldly moves forward into each new era of life.

### ACT ON IT

- What are you clinging to that is holding you back or is no longer useful? There could be a sport or instrument that's no longer right for you, it could be a relationship that just isn't working, it could be boyhood itself. Whatever it is for you, resolve to let it go.

- Who do you need to forgive? Who do you need to ask forgiveness of? After you've decided, you know what to do.

- Use the toggles to decide which traits you need most as you go up against the biggest challenge you're facing in your life, right now.

**ACHIEVEMENT UNLOCKED!**
**LEVEL III COMPLETE!**

You are a child of the universe,
no less than the trees and the stars;
you have a right to be here.
And whether or not it is clear to you,
no doubt the universe is unfolding as it should.

—MAX EHRMANN,
*DESIDERATA*

# CONGRATULATIONS! TRUE WARRIOR RANKING ACHIEVED!

There you go, kid. You've made it.

You've got your Warrior manual and your rite of passage for manhood, all in one. This is everything you need to be a powerful—and honorable—man in our world.

In Phase III of your training, you learned how to call out toxic traits when you testified in front of US senators, defending those who needed defending. And you put a cherry on top of the sundae when you stole a naval warship, letting go of everything holding you back as you sailed off into the sunset (err . . . sunrise).

With these accomplishments, I actually can't call you "kid" anymore. You've become a True Warrior. I'm incredibly proud to know you. You are a good man and a real man *in the same moment*. You are as fierce as you are kind. Tough as you are gentle. Sometimes vulnerable and sometimes ruthless. You can handle yourself in the wild, and you can defend your tribe. You've risen to the ranks of True Warrior, and I'd be stoked to have you in my army any day of the week. And so would a lot of people.

I still think it would be rad if we could spear fight by firelight in the Serengeti. If we could, this would be that moment I was talking about in Challenge 1. This is when you'd outskill and outmaneuver me. You'd bash the spear out of my hands and I'd fall to the dirt, coughing in the dust. Hyenas would laugh, but this time, you'd turn to them and they'd run in terror, just at the sight of you. They know a True Warrior when they see one.

I'd pick myself up and smile, proud of your newfound abilities, and proud of you as my Warrior mentee. Only thing? As of right now, you're no longer my mentee. You're my equal, a fellow True Warrior.

# LET GO OF YOUR WARRIOR GUIDE

Seriously, it gives me chills thinking about what a freaking awesome human you've become. I'm so pumped for what you're going to do next. I'm legitimately tearing up over here. Am I making it awkward for you? Good.

We've been through some wild adventures together, right? While this is where we part ways, we can still cherish how we influenced each other. Writing this has made a huge difference in my own Warrior journey. Thanks for breathing life into me.

I'd give you a hug goodbye if I could, but I'm still trapped in this book. The good news is that you can come back any time you need to. Reread chapters, study your notes, go through the resources in the back.

But before we go, there remains one task to seal your Warrior designation and make your new rank official. . . .

# DECIDE TO JOIN THE TRIBE

Maybe it never occurred to you, but there's a whole family of other True Warriors out there. They're seriously everywhere. They may not have gone through this exact training, but they're out there, living life on these terms. Now that you know what you're looking for, you'll be able to spot them. You'll know them when you meet them. And here's a clue: Women are at least half of them—probably more than half, in fact!

Band together and help one another improve. Every Warrior can learn *something* from every other Warrior. Plus every master was once a beginner and every master knows they can always improve their mastery. Your last task is to leave me here, depart your training grounds, and go find your fellows on the battleground, where you can improve your skills, together. It's one thing to know this stuff in a book. It's a whole different thing to act on it in the wilderness of your hometown.

So go. Use your training. Put it to use in our action-packed real world where it's needed most. It's a beautiful, terrible, magnificent landscape we get to play in. Because of that, some of the Warriors you'll meet will be advanced beyond even our combined understanding. And you'll meet some aspiring Warriors whom you may be able to mentor along their journeys. Still others may be fallen Warriors and really struggling. Shoulder them.

But no matter what, *join them*. That's how you take your training completion award and really earn it.

Don't worry, you don't have to be perfect out there. It would take multiple lifetimes to get all this stuff exactly right. As long as you're working toward these things, a little at a time, even with baby steps (like I have to), you remain in the Warrior class.

But your very first step, right now? It's toward the King of Beasts. It's your time.

Cry your battle cry, lift your weapon into the sky, and charge.

*The boy who is prepared to navigate all challenges with honor? That is a man indeed.*

You're ready, Warrior. Go slay that King of Beasts.

# RESOURCES

## HOW TO CREATE YOUR OWN RITE OF PASSAGE

If you're interested in creating a real-life rite of passage, here are the five required components. For crafting your very own "man-defining" adventure, you must choose something that's:

### 1. DIFFICULT

Your rite of passage *has* to be hard. You need to choose something you *think* you can do, but you're not quite sure how. That way, you'll be thrown curveballs along the way. It's in the struggle that you will grow. Success may require multiple attempts. If you know you won't make mistakes, keep looking. A well-selected rite will make you ridiculously proud of completing it because of how challenging it will be. A rite doesn't need to be expensive, but raising or earning sufficient funds could be a part of the experience.

### 2. RELEVANT

Shoving your hand into a glove full of bullet ants probably has no purpose for your life. What's something that *is* relevant to you? Does your family have a sport, activity, destination, or tradition? What's the "ultimate" experience for the thing or things that you're already passionate about? What sounds freaking awesome to you?

## 3. PURPOSEFUL

The awesomeness of the activity you choose is *not* the endgame. The point is who you'll become in the process. The activity is the tool to take you from one place to another as a man. You must decide, in advance, what the experience will mean to you. What do you want answered? What values and character traits do you want to adopt? How will doing this thing help you believe that you can handle whatever comes your way and protect your tribe?

## 4. GUIDED

You need an experienced guide. Rites should never be solo efforts, despite including elements of independence. Even Australian Aboriginal boys received guided training before their desert survival. So who will train you? Is there an adventure guide outfitter, coach, instructor, or leader who can help to prepare you? In addition to the guide for the activity, you should have a separate parent or adult who will help to discuss the values and lessons you've learned along the way.

## 5. FUN!

What would make your rite of passage something you will never forget? Are there any Battle Crew members who could make the journey even better? Invite them! Collaborate and create a multiactivity adventure! If this is something you need to undertake only with your guide and parent, then ask them to collaborate with you for making it the adventure of a lifetime.

### EXAMPLES:

You organize a nonviolent protest of your city's or state's environmental policies, then set a goal to plant a thousand trees with your protesters!

Your family hires a mountain-climbing guide service to summit a mountain, such as Whitney, Rainier, Washington, or Denali.

You spearhead a campaign to increase mental-health awareness at your school.

You attend a weeklong music camp with the goal of playing the hardest song you can imagine mastering.

You build a solar-powered phone and device-charging station for your school's courtyard or common area.

You and your four best friends go on a trip where each of you chooses and plans a half-day activity. Set a price cap that everyone can afford. Example weekend: Friend 1 organizes a trip to an action archery course. Friend 2 arranges a graffiti cover-up paint project. Friend 3 finds a whitewater-rafting excursion with a group rate. Friend 4 chooses to volunteer to serve food in a homeless shelter. Friend 5 wants to learn some sweet dance moves to crush it on the dance floor and sets up a lesson. With creative thinking, planning, deal-hunting, negotiation, and adult guidance, you could make something similar into an affordable reality!

These are simply for your inspiration. Ultimately, as long as all five components are included, the awesomeness of your rite of passage is limited only by your creativity, imagination, and grit.

# HOW TO FIND A
# QUALITY THERAPIST

If you're a young man or caring adult who is searching for a therapist . . . then congratulations! It's an awesome and courageous life decision to see a therapist regularly. However, just as there are good teachers and bad teachers, and amazing athletes and meh athletes, it's the same with mental health professionals. Here are steps for finding someone who is the right fit for you:

## STEP 1: DECIDE WHERE TO START

There's a difference between a therapist, psychologist, and psychiatrist. They work toward the same goal but have different ways of getting there. All three can work together to help you as a team, but it's up to you to choose the way that's best for you.

**PSYCHOLOGIST:** This is a doctor who specializes in understanding thought patterns and how those patterns affect our behaviors, moods, and feelings. Psychologists don't prescribe medications. Their sessions are typically fifty to ninety minutes. This time is focused on you and what's going on in your life. It's 100 percent private, and psychologists aren't allowed to talk about the specifics of your sessions, or they'd lose their jobs (except in cases of abuse, which they are required to report to authorities).

**PSYCHIATRIST:** This is a doctor who specializes in diagnosing and treating mental illnesses and conditions. These doctors can prescribe medications that help your mind to function in a healthier way. Their sessions are typically fifteen to thirty minutes and very often result in a prescription for medication.

**THERAPIST:** This is any trained professional—doctor or not—who helps their patients clarify feelings and make decisions, all while offering support and guidance. A therapist could be a psychologist or psychiatrist. But therapists can also be licensed professional counselors, social workers, or certified life coaches.

I chose to start with a therapist and psychologist because I didn't like the idea of medications. Now I also have a psychiatrist and a light dosage of a medication that's beneficial for me. I still visit a psychologist on a monthly basis, kind of like checking in with a doctor for a follow-up appointment. That's what's right for me. But you? You are different. So do what's right for you!

## STEP 2: DECIDE WHICH STYLE OF THERAPY IS RIGHT FOR YOU

I was dealing with the trauma of witnessing multiple fatalities. Because of that, I wanted to find someone who was a pro in a style of therapy called EMDR. That, combined with Cognitive Behavorial Therapy (often called CBT), was what helped me to redefine the negative messages I had created in my head as a result of those traumas.

You can Google what those letters mean if you like, but it would be better to research the style of therapy that's the best fit for what *you* are dealing with.

So ask yourself: Is it anxiety? Substance abuse? Niceness and people-pleasing? Difficulty expressing anger? Depression? Loneliness? Relationship problems? Whatever it is, talk to a trusted adult in your life about searching for "What kind of therapist is best for dealing with _____."

## STEP 3: SELECT A HANDFUL OF SPECIFIC PROFESSIONALS

Next up, choose from three to five potential options for therapist. Like all relationships, you don't just want to go with the first option. You want to find the best fit.

*Psychology Today* has a great directory of therapists, as does Google Maps. They even have user ratings! Select a few who specialize in treating what you're dealing with.

If the internet turns out to be a dead end, your school counselor can get you started, as can an abuse hotline (even if you're not dealing with abuse). You can also ask a friend who sees a good therapist. (In fact, simply asking your friends will probably help them to feel more at ease with their own healing journey. It tells them that they are not alone.)

## STEP 4: GRILL 'EM

Now that you've got three to five options, you're gonna grill 'em and figure out if they're a good fit for you.

Some therapists may require an appointment. Some may speak with you over the phone before meeting. Either way, respect how they prefer to meet for the first time. Whatever they desire, give them a third-degree interrogation. Make it clear that you will not open up unless you believe they can handle you at your toughest and roughest. Ask them every objection you have. Like this:

**What makes you—a total stranger to me—think that you could possibly help me?**

**Have you ever actually helped someone like me before? Tell me about it.**

**One of your patients gave you a three-star review. How do you respond to what they said?**

**What made you want to become a therapist in the first place?**

**Doesn't it suck to listen to people whine and complain all day?**

**Your qualifications are from reading a bunch of textbooks and getting a piece of paper to put on your wall. How can that help with the real-life stuff I'm dealing with?**

Those questions might sound harsh, but if a therapist can't answer them, or they're upset by them in any way, then that person doesn't deserve to know the deepest parts of your story.

But what if they aren't shaken and answer your questions in a way that makes sense to you? What if you start to think that there's an opportunity for a connection? That's when it's up to you to commit. And, if at any point along the way this feels difficult or overwhelming, keep reaching out to that trusted adult for support or advice.

## STEP 5: MAKE A COMMITMENT

The final step, after your therapist has proven themselves worthy, is to prove yourself worthy of them. You've got to make the choice to do the work. Trust me, there will be times when you don't want to go. In fact, if you're like me, you'll sabotage your own appointments, maybe without even realizing it. (Hint: It's called avoidance!) Doing the work means that the deepest part of you commits to opening up at your appointments and taking that time seriously.

You can also take therapy supplements. Just like drinking a protein powder smoothie after a workout can maximize your gains, there are ways to maximize your therapy sessions. These include meditation, reading books that your therapist recommends (ya gotta ask), listening to podcasts about the thing you're dealing with (there are awesome podcasts on every mental health issue out there), and joining groups of people who are dealing with what you're dealing with (in person or online can both be helpful).

There you have it. Your five steps to getting quality therapy that's right for you. Get to it.

# HELP WITH LIFE'S TOUGH STUFF

If you're dealing with, or might be dealing with, any of the following, these free hotlines are 100 percent anonymous. You don't even have to give your name. I highly recommend calling if you have even a suspicion that you should. Most are open 24/7, 365 days a year. That means you can ask for help at ANY time. Also provided are links to find therapists. Your school very likely has a mental health counselor you can speak with as well.

## ANY KIND OF CRISIS
CrisisChat: Crisischat.org
Crisis Text Line: Text HOME to 741741 or crisistextline.org
Girls & Boys Town National Hotline: 800-448-3000

## EMOTIONAL ABUSE, MENTAL ABUSE, VERBAL ABUSE, AND/OR PHYSICAL ABUSE
National Domestic Violence Hotline: 800-799-SAFE (7233)
or thehotline.org/help
psychologytoday.com/us/therapists/domestic-violence

## SEXUAL ASSAULT, RAPE, AND/OR SEXUAL VIOLENCE
Rape, Sexual Assault, Abuse, and Incest National Network (RAINN): 800-656-HOPE
National Domestic Violence Hotline (Child Abuse/Sexual Abuse): 800-799-7233 or thehotline.org
psychologytoday.com/us/therapists/sexual-abuse

## SUICIDE
Suicide Prevention: 800-273-8255 or online chat at suicidepreventionlifeline.org/chat
psychologytoday.com/us/therapists/suicidal-ideation

## CHILD ABUSE
Childhelp National Child Abuse Hotline: 800-422-4453 or childhelp.org/hotline

## EATING DISORDERS

National Eating Disorders Center Helpline: 800-931-2237 or
nationaleatingdisorders.org/help-support/contact-helpline

## ALCOHOL ABUSE

Al-Anon for Families of Alcoholics: meeting information at
800-344-2666 or al-anon.org
Families Anonymous: 800-736-9805 or familiesanonymous.org
SAMHSA National Helpline: 800-662-HELP (4357) or samhsa.gov/
find-help/national-helpline

## DRUG ABUSE

National Institute on Drug Abuse Hotline: 800-662-4357
or drugabuse.gov
Cocaine Anonymous: 800-347-8998 or ca.org

Asking for help is one of the most courageous things a man can do.

# SOURCES

## CHALLENGE 1: HAMISI & DECIDE TO STEP UP

Hamisi, Kakuta. "Facing the Lion." Maasai Association. Accessed January 3, 2020. maasai-association.org/lion.html

Hamisi, Kakuta. Interview by author, Nairobi, Kenya, May 2019.

Hamisi, Kakuta. "Maasai Warrior Training Experience." Maasai Camp. Accessed January 3, 2020. maasaicamp.com/warriorcamp.html

Paoletti, Gabe. "The Excruciating Bullet Ant Glove Test of the Mawé People." All That's Interesting. Accessed January 3, 2020. allthatsinteresting.com/bullet-ant-glove

Masters, Robert Augustus. *To Be a Man: A Guide to True Masculine Power.* Boulder, CO: Sounds True, 2015.

McLaughlin, Rhett, and Neal, Link. Ep. 69 Rhett & Link "Most Bizarre Rites of Passage." Ear Biscuits. Audio podcast. podcasts.apple.com/us/podcast/ep-69-rhett-link-most-bizarre-rites-of-passage-ear-biscuits/id717407884?i=1000342264689

McKay, Brett, and McKay, Kate. "Coming of Age: The Importance of Male Rites of Passage." *The Art of Manliness.* November 9, 2008; last updated November 16, 2017. artofmanliness.com/articles/coming-of-age-the-importance-of-male-rites-of-passage

McKay, Brett, and McKay, Kate. "8 Interesting (and Insane) Male Rites of Passages from Around the World." *The Art of Manliness.* February 21, 2010; last updated November 2, 2018. artofmanliness.com/articles/male-rites-of-passage-from-around-the-world

McKay, Brett. "Podcast #505: A Man's Need for Ritual." The Art of Manliness. Audio podcast. May 6, 2019; last updated January 5, 2020. artofmanliness.com/articles/mens-rituals-rites-of-passage

Alexander, Bobby C., and Norbeck, Edward. "Rite of Passage." *Encyclopedia Britannica.* Accessed January 3, 2020. britannica.com/topic/rite-of-passage

"Ouch! The Insect Sting Pain Scale | Explaining the Schmidt Sting Pain Index." Terminix. Accessed January 3, 2020. terminix.com/blog/science-nature/the-insect-sting-pain-scale

Ingolfsland, Jason. "25 Crazy Rites of Passage." List25. May 6, 2019. list25.com/25-crazy-rites-of-passage

Obama, Barack. *Dreams from My Father: A Story of Race and Inheritance.* New York: Three Rivers Press, 2004.

## CHALLENGE 2: WAY & BECOME SELF-AWARE

Way, Danny. *Waiting for Lightning*. Directed by Jacob Rosenberg. Culver City: Samuel Goldwyn Films, 2012.

Way, Danny. "I Am Danny Way, Parts 1–5." YouTube video series, May 2011. youtube.com/watch?v=esgAWtFXsMo

Kotler, Steven. *The Rise of Superman: Decoding the Science of Ultimate Human Performance*. New York: New Harvest, 2014.

Rothman, Tibby. "Danny Way, the World's Best Skateboarder, Gets a New Documentary." *Los Angeles Times*. December 6, 2012. laweekly.com/danny-way-the-worlds-best -skateboarder-gets-a-new-documentary

"Danny Way Jumps Great Wall July 9." *Transworld Skateboarding*. July 8, 2005. skate-boarding.transworld.net/news/danny-way-jumps-great-wall-july-9

Skateboarder. "15 Things: The Great Wall." *Men's Journal*. Accessed January 3, 2020. adventuresportsnetwork.com/sport/skateboarding/15thngsgretwal

Johnston, Bret Anthony. "Danny Way and the Gift of Fear." *Men's Journal*. January 2, 2013. mensjournal.com/features/danny-way-and-the-gift-of-fear-20130102

Michna, Ian. "The Danny Way Interview." *Jenkem*. January 17, 2013. jenkemmag.com/home/2013/01/17/the-danny-way-interview

Storoni, Mithu. *Stress Proof: The Scientific Solution to Protect Your Brain and Body—and Be More Resilient Every Day*. New York: TarcherPerigee, 2017.

Storoni, Mithu. "This 2-Minute Breathing Exercise Can Help You Make Better Decisions, According to a New Study." *Inc*. July 4, 2019. inc.com/mithu-storoni/this-2-minute-breathing-exercise-can-help-you-make-better-decisions-according-to-a-new-study.html

Johnson, C.; Burke, C.; Brinkman, S.; and Wade, T. "Effectiveness of a School-Based Mindfulness Program for Transdiagnostic Prevention in Young Adolescents." National Center for Biotechnology Information. March 21, 2016. ncbi.nlm.nih.gov/pubmed/27054828

Singer, Michael A. *The Untethered Soul: The Journey Beyond Yourself*. Oakland: New Harbinger Publications/Noetic Books, 2007.

Lynch, David. "Center for Health and Wellness." The David Lynch Foundation. Accessed January 3, 2020. davidlynchfoundation.org

Storoni, Mithu. *The Science of Breathing and Its Importance in Yoga*. Directed by Mark Heley. An Uplift Production.

*The Science Behind Yoga*. Directed by Damian Jordan, Mark Heley, Chris Deckker, Emma-Lee Luther, Jonathan Fae, Stefanos Ioannidis, and Ayana Levy. An Uplift Production.

Marcus, Aubrey. *Own the Day, Own Your Life: Optimized Practices for Waking, Working, Learning, Eating, Training, Playing, Sleeping, and Sex*. New York: Harper Wave, 2018.

Headspace, Inc. "Headspace: Meditation & Sleep." Apple App Store, (2019). apps.apple.com/us/app/headspace-meditation-sleep/id493145008

## CHALLENGE 3: HOLLENBECK & SHIFT YOUR FINISH LINE

Hollenbeck, Dennis. Interview by author, Henderson, NV, June 2019.

Hollenbeck, Dennis. *Dust to Glory*. Directed by Dana Brown. Dana Brown Films, in association with SCORE International and BCII. 2005.

Hollenbeck, Dennis. *Dust 2 Glory.* Directed by Dana Brown. Dana Brown Films, in association with SCORE International and BCII, 2018.

Casa Esperanza. "Mexico—Casa Esperanza" Calvary Relief International. Accessed January 3, 2020. calvaryreliefint.com/mexico-casa-esperanza

Comic Drake. "What Makes Someone Worthy of Thor's Hammer? (Mjolnir)." YouTube video, posted December 23, 2016. youtube.com/watch?v=-I7qXoB-KSc

Hedash, Kara. "Female Thor Explained: How Jane Foster Became Worthy." *ScreenRant.* July 21, 2019. screenrant.com/female-thor-explained-jane-foster-comics-origin-powers

Manson, Mark. *The Subtle Art of Not Giving a F\*ck: A Counterintuitive Approach to Living a Good Life.* New York: Harper, 2016.

Hemmann, Steve. Interview by author, August 2019.

## ACHIEVEMENT UNLOCKED! LEVEL 1 COMPLETE!

Frazee, Gretchen, and Morales, Patty Gorena. "Suicide Among Teens and Young Adults Reaches Highest Level Since 2000." *PBS News Hour.* June 18, 2019. pbs.org/newshour/nation/suicide-among-teens-and-young-adults-reaches-highest-level-since-2000

Evans, Sean. "Not Talking About Mental Health Is Literally Killing Men." *Men's Health.* June 6, 2019. menshealth.com/uk/mental-strength/a27785395/men-mental-health-awareness-month

Nett, Sandra. Interview by author, December 2014.

*Final Fantasy II.* Super NES Video Game. Directed by Hironobu Sakaguchi. July 19, 1991. Tokyo: Square/Square Enix.

Mitchell, Morgan. Interview by author, December 2014–January 2015.

## CHALLENGE 4: STIRBU & REINFORCE YOUR ARMOR

Stirbu, Viorel "Wally." Interview by author, Carstensz Pyramid, Indonesia, 2015.

Stirbu, Viorel "Wally." Interview by author. Lyle, WA, USA, July 2019.

Birch, Adelyn. *Boundaries After a Pathological Relationship.* Seattle: Amazon, 2014.

Cloud, Henry, and Townsend, John. *Boundaries: When to Say Yes, How to Say No to Take Control of Your Life.* Grand Rapids, MI: Zondervan, 1992.

Gillingham, John. "Brémule, Battle Of." Encyclopedia.com. Updated December 2019. encyclopedia.com/history/encyclopedias-almanacs-transcripts-and-maps/bremule-battle

"Top 10 Strangest Battles of the Middle Ages." Medievalists.net. Accessed January 3, 2020. medievalists.net/2014/08/top-10-strangest-battles-middle-ages/

Rosenberg, Marshall B. *Nonviolent Communication: A Language of Life: Life-Changing Tools for Healthy Relationships.* Encinitas, CA: PuddleDancer Press, 2015.

Mason, Paul T., and Kreger, Randi. *Stop Walking on Eggshells: Taking Your Life Back When Someone You Care About Has Borderline Personality Disorder.* Oakland, CA: New Harbinger Publications, 2015.

Rapson, James, and English, Craig. *Anxious to Please: 7 Revolutionary Practices for the Chronically Nice.* Naperville, IL: Sourcebooks, 2006.

Thomas, Shannon. *Healing from Hidden Abuse: A Journey Through the Stages of Recovery from Psychological Abuse.* Tempe, AZ: MAST Publishing House, 2016.

Rosenberg, Ross. *The Human Magnet Syndrome: Why We Love People Who Hurt Us.* Dublin, Ireland: Premier Publishing & Media, 2013.

Brown, Brené. *The Gifts of Imperfection: Let Go of Who You Think You're Supposed to Be and Embrace Who You Are*. Center City, MN: Hazelden Publishing, 2017.

Brown, Brené. *Rising Strong: How the Ability to Reset Transforms the Way We Live, Love, Parent, and Lead*. New York: Random House, 2017.

Funk, Jessie. Interview by author, October 2019.

Cloud, Henry, and Townsend, John. "Wise Men [and Women] Bring Gifts of Boundaries at the Holidays." Episode #4 of For the Love of Fall & Holidays series with Jen Hatmaker. For the Love. Audio podcast. podcasts.apple.com/sg/podcast/dr-henry-cloud-john-townsend-wise-men-women-bring-gifts/id1258388821?i=1000397153404

Glickman, Charlie. "Boundaries vs. Ultimatums." Make Sex Easy. Accessed January 3, 2020. makesexeasy.com/boundaries-vs-ultimatums

*Halo*. Xbox Video Game. Directed by Jason Jones. November 15, 2001. Microsoft Game Studios, MacSoft. Redmond, WA.

Glover, Robert A. *No More Mr. Nice Guy: A Proven Plan for Getting What You Want in Love, Sex, and Life*. Kindle Edition. Philadelphia: Running Press, 2003.

Gazupura, Aziz. *Not Nice: Stop People Pleasing, Staying Silent, & Feeling Guilty . . . and Start Speaking Up, Saying No, Asking Boldly, and Unapologetically Being Yourself*. Seattle: Amazon, 2017.

## CHALLENGE 5: JORGESON & CHOOSE YOUR BATTLE CREW

Caldwell, Tommy. *The Push: A Climber's Search for the Path*. New York: Penguin, 2018.

Caldwell, Tommy. *Reel Rock 6*. Directed by Anson Fogel, Josh Lowell, Peter Mortimer, and Nick Rosen. Big Up Productions & Sender Films, 2011.

Jorgeson, Kevin, and Caldwell, Tommy. *Progression*. Directed by Bret Lowell, Josh Lowell, and Cooper Roberts. Big Up Productions & Sender Films, 2009.

Jorgeson, Kevin. "The Dawn Wall: The Long Struggle for the World's Hardest Big-Wall Free Climb." American Alpine Club. 2015. publications.americanalpineclub.org/articles/13201213305/The-Dawn-Wall

Jorgeson, Kevin, and Caldwell, Tommy. *The Dawn Wall*. Directed by Josh Lowell and Peter Mortimer. Red Bull Films, Red Bull Media House, in association with Sender Films. 2017.

Davies, Dave. "'It Looked Impossible': New Film Follows Free Climbers up the 'Dawn Wall.'" NPR. November 20, 2018. npr.org/2018/11/20/669573056/dawn-wall-climbers-gripped-razor-thin-edges-up-el-capitans-impossible-face

Carpenter, Hayden. "What 'The Dawn Wall' Left Out." Outside Online. September 18, 2018. outsideonline.com/2344706/dawn-wall-documentary-tommy-caldwell-review

Patagonia. "Tommy Caldwell Climbing Pitch 15—The Dawn Wall." YouTube video, posted January 19, 2015. youtube.com/watch?v=PLd_c4CjG44

Bisharat, Andrew. "Dawn Wall's Underdog Climber Recounts His Push to Catch Up." *National Geographic*. January 13, 2015. nationalgeographic.com/news/2015/1/140111-interview-kevin-jorgeson-dawn-wall-yosemite-adventure/#close

Quinn, Neely. "TBP 027: Kevin Jorgeson Talks about the Dawn Wall and Highballs." The TrainingBeta Podcast: Climbing Training Podcast, Audio podcast. July 9, 2015. podcasts.apple.com/us/podcast/tbp-027-kevin-jorgeson-talks-about-dawn-wall-highballs/id827233918?i=1000346802667

Goradia, Kevin, and Eakin, Amanda. "Kevin Jorgeson." To Hell and Back. Audio podcast. archive.org/details/podcast_to-hell-back_kevin-jorgeson_1000382228504

"Life and Climbs of Kevin Jorgeson, The." The Firn Line. January 11, 2019. podcasts.apple. com/us/podcast/the-life-and-climbs-of-kevin-jorgeson/id1191897461?i=1000427427504

National Geographic. "World's Hardest Climb Goal of Yosemite Wall Climber." YouTube video, posted January 15, 2015. youtube.com/watch?v=l_lZc7nATT4

Michler, Ryan. "Protect, Provide, Preside." Order of Man: Reclaiming and Restoring Masculinity. Audio podcast. podcasts.apple.com/us/podcast/order-of-man-protect-provide-preside/id979752171

Burkus, David. "You're NOT the Average of the Five People You Surround Yourself With." Mission.org. May 23, 2018. medium.com/the-mission/youre-not-the-average-of-the-five-people-you-surround-yourself-with-f21b817f6e69

Hemmann, Steve. Interview by author, August 2019.

Thomas, Shannon, LPCW. Interview by author, October 2019.

ESPN. "Lyon College Players Shave Heads to Support OC." August 28, 2019. espn.com/college-football/story/_/id/27480758/lyon-college-players-shave-heads-support-oc

## CHALLENGE 6: SHACKLETON & GET GRITTY

Shackleton, Ernest. *South: The* Endurance *Expedition.* New York: Signet Books, 1999.

*The* Endurance: *Shackleton's Legendary Antarctic Expedition.* Directed by George Butler. Discover Channel Pictures et al. 2001.

The Explorer's Club. "'Shackleton: Death or Glory' Featuring Hon. Alexandra Shackleton and Tim Jarvis." Vimeo online video. April 15, 2015. vimeo.com/125077953

Alexander, Caroline. *The* Endurance: *Shackleton's Legendary Antarctic Expedition.* New York: Knopf, 1998.

Arbuckle, Alex Q. "1914–1916: The *Endurance:* Survival Against the Greatest Odds." Mashable. Accessed January 3, 2019. mashable.com/2015/10/10/the-endurance

"Sir Ernest Shackleton, *Endurance* Voyage Timeline and Map." Cool Antarctica. Accessed January 3, 2019. coolantarctica.com/Antarctica%20fact%20file/History/Ernest_ Shackleton_map_time_line.php

Climer, Amy. "5 Elements of Shackleton's Leadership." Climer Consulting. December 15, 2016. climerconsulting.com/five-elements-shackletons-leadership

Laozi. *Tao Te Ching.* Translated by Gia-fu Feng and Jane English. New York: Vintage Books, 1972.

Viesturs, Ed, with Roberts, David. *No Shortcuts to the Top: Climbing the World's 14 Highest Peaks.* New York: Broadway Books, 2007.

## ACHIEVEMENT UNLOCKED! LEVEL II COMPLETE!

Rochman, Bonnie. "The Results Are In: First National Study of Teen Masturbation." *Time.* August 11, 2011. healthland.time.com/2011/08/11/boys-masturbate-more-than-girls-seriously

"80% of boys masturbate by 17."

Robbins, Cynthia L.; Schick, Vanessa; Reece, Michael; et al. "Prevalence, Frequency, and Associations of Masturbation With Partnered Sexual Behaviors Among US Adolescents." JAMA Network. December 2011. jamanetwork.com/journals/jamapediatrics/fullarticle/1107656

Jacques, Renee. "11 Reasons You Should Be Having More Orgasms." *HuffPost.* Updated December 6, 2017. huffpost.com/entry/orgasm-health-benefits_n_4143213

Travers, Colleen. "7 Not-So-Obvious Health Benefits of Having an Orgasm." *Fitness Magazine.* Accessed January 3, 2020. fitnessmagazine.com/mind-body/sex/benefits-of-orgasm

Zoldan, Rachel Jacoby. "14 Benefits of Female Masturbation and Why Every Woman Should Do It." *Self.* December 31, 2018. self.com/story/13-reasons-every-woman-should-masturbate-besides-the-obvious

Tschinkel, Arielle. "12 Unexpected Health Benefits of Orgasms." *Business Insider.* Last updated March 1, 2019. businessinsider.sg/orgasm-health-benefits-2018-11

Henriques, Sasha. Interview by author, April 2019.

Thomas, Shannon. Interview by author, October 2019.

Sargent, Sara. Interview by author, December 2019.

Elizabeth, Lindsay. "The Average Age a Child First Sees Pornography Is Shockingly Younger Than You'd Think." *Faithwire.* April 4, 2018. faithwire.com/2018/04/04/the-average-age-a-child-first-sees-pornography-is-shockingly-younger-than-youd-think

Warner, Russ. "The Detrimental Effects of Pornography on Small Children." *Net Nanny.* December 19, 2017. netnanny.com/blog/the-detrimental-effects-of-pornography-on-small-children

"What's the Average Age of a Child's First Exposure to Porn?" *Fight the New Drug.* August 20, 2019. fightthenewdrug.org/real-average-age-of-first-exposure

Sliwa, Jim. "Age of First Exposure to Pornography Shapes Men's Attitudes Toward Women." American Psychological Association. August 3, 2017. apa.org/news/press/releases/2017/08/pornography-exposure

Fight the New Drug. *Brain Heart World.* November 1, 2018. fightthenewdrug.org

"How Porn Can Become Addictive." *Fight the New Drug.* August 23, 2017. fightthenewdrug.org/how-porn-can-become-addictive

"How Porn Can Damage Consumers' Sex Lives." *Fight the New Drug.* August 23, 2017. fightthenewdrug.org/how-porn-damages-consumers-sex-lives

"3 Surprising Secrets the Porn Industry Hides from Consumers." *Fight the New Drug.* October 28, 2019. fightthenewdrug.org/porn-industry-doesnt-want-know

"How Watching Porn Turned Me into the Worst Guy in Bed." *Fight the New Drug.* August 21, 2018. fightthenewdrug.org/i-thought-porn-would-make-me-great-in-bed-but-it-did-the-opposite

Porter, Tony. "A Call to Men." TedWomen 2010. ted.com/talks/tony_porter_a_call_to_men

"Google's Alan Eustace Beats Baumgartner's Skydiving Record." BBC News. October 24, 2014. bbc.com/news/world-us-canada-29766189

"Tea Consent." Blue Seat Studios. YouTube video, posted November 16, 2015. youtube.com/watch?v=oQbei5JGiT8

"Violent Sexpectations for Virgins: What Hardcore Porn Is Teaching Our Generation." *Fight the New Drug.* August 13, 2019. fightthenewdrug.org/30-year-old-virgins-what-watching-porn-is-doing-to-peoples-sex-lives

Murray, Terri. "Myth-Busting the Pornography Industry's Propaganda." *Conatus News.* October 13, 2017. conatusnews.com/myth-busting-pornography-propaganda

Reichert, Michael C. *How to Raise a Boy: The Power of Connection to Build Good Men.* New York: TarcherPerigee, 2019.

# CHALLENGE 7: CREWS & CARRY ANTIVENOM

Crews, Terry. *Manhood: How to Be a Better Man—or Just Live with One.* Toronto: Zinc Ink, 2014.

Crews, Terry. Hotboxin' with Mike Tyson, part 1. Audio podcast. podcasts.apple.com/us/podcast/terry-crews-part-1/id1449316560?i=1000456119222

Crews, Terry. Hotboxin' with Mike Tyson, part 2. Audio podcast. podcasts.apple.com/us/podcast/terry-crews-part-2/id1449316560?i=1000456118817

Crews, Terry. "Terry Crews complete opening statement." C-SPAN. YouTube video, posted June 26, 2018. youtube.com/watch?v=ZtI4eH1U2rY

"Rise Above: How Amanda Nguyen Used Her Sexual Assault to Help Millions." *Money.* YouTube video, posted June 13, 2019. youtube.com/watch?v=PwauKlmByFI

"Be Fearless: Amanda Nguyen and Rise." The Case Foundation. YouTube video, posted July 2, 2019. youtube.com/watch?v=YKgbWhPk9G8

Klich, Tanya. "Rise CEO Amanda Nguyen on Launching a Civil Rights Startup That Fights for Rape Survivors." Forbes.com. March 8, 2019. forbes.com/sites/tanyaklich/2019/03/08/rise-ceo-amanda-nguyen-on-launching-a-civil-rights-startup-that-fights-for-rape-survivors/#1281e49f1d01

Nguyen, Amanda. "Rise Justice Labs." Risenow. Accessed January 3, 2020. risenow.us

Alter, Charlotte. "Here's What Happens When You Get a Rape Kit Exam." *Time.* Last updated July 22, 2014. time.com/3001467/heres-what-happens-when-you-get-a-rape-kit-exam

Walsh, Dylan. "A Moral and Economic Argument for Testing Rape Kits." Stanford Graduate School of Business. February 16, 2018. gsb.stanford.edu/insights/moral-economic-argument-testing-rape-kits

"What Is a Sexual Assault Forensic Exam?" RAINN. Accessed January 3, 2019. rainn.org/articles/rape-kit

"Break the Rules Like . . . Amanda Nguyen." *Unladylike.* August 21, 2018. unladylike.co/blog/2018/8/21/break-the-rules-like-amanda-nguyen

Gajanan, Mahita. "'This Happened to Me Too.' Terry Crews Details His Alleged Sexual Assault During Emotional Senate Testimony." *Time.* June 26, 2018. time.com/5322629/terry-crews-sexual-assault-senate-committee

"Sexual Assault Survivors' Rights Act." C-Span. June 26, 2018. www.c-span.org/video/?447596-1/terry-crews-testifies-survivors-bill-rights

Budd, Zach. "5 Reasons the #MeToo Movement Got an Epic Boost." *Medium.* July 5, 2018. medium.com/sexposblog/5-reasons-the-metoo-movement-got-an-epic-boost-cbfcae1e9046

Ali, Rasha. "Terry Crews to D. L. Hughley: 'Are You Implying I "Wanted" to Be Sexually Assaulted?'" *USA Today.* January 28, 2019. usatoday.com/story/life/people/2019/01/28/terry-crews-celebs-mocked-his-sexual-assault-metoo-movement-dl-hughley-50-cent/2699273002

Sapi, Eva. "Lyme Disease Research Group." University of New Haven. Accessed January 3, 2019. newhaven.edu/research/labs-groups/lyme-disease.php

Hill, Kyle. "The Most Poisonous/Venomous Animals in the World." *Science-Based Life.* April 12, 2011. sciencebasedlife.wordpress.com/2011/04/12/the-most-poisonousvenomous-animals-in-the-world

"Protecting Your Children: Advice from Child Molesters." Vermont Department of Children and Families. Accessed January 3, 2019. dcf.vermont.gov/sites/dcf/files/Prevention/docs/Protecting-Children.pdf

Hammel-Zabin, Amy. "The Mind of a Child Molester." *Psychology Today.* Last reviewed June 9, 2016. psychologytoday.com/us/articles/200307/the-mind-child-molester

RAINN. "Children and Teens: Statistics: Child Sexual Abuse Is a Widespread Problem." Accessed January 3, 2020. rainn.org/statistics/children-and-teens

RAINN. "Victims of Sexual Violence: Statistics: Sexual Violence Affects Millions of Americans." Accessed January 3, 2020. rainn.org/statistics/victims-sexual-violence

National Sexual Violence Resource Center—Info & Stats for Journalists. "Statistics About Sexual Violence." Accessed January 3, 2020. nsvrc.org/sites/default/files/publications_nsvrc_factsheet_media-packet_statistics-about-sexual-violence_0.pdf

"Protecting Your Children: Advice from Child Molesters," op. cit.

"One Sex Offender's Strategy." Spaz.ca. Accessed January 3, 2020. spaz.ca/aaron/billious/RCYS/Chapter22.html

Tull, Matthew. "Delayed-Onset PTSD Symptoms." Verywell Mind. Updated September 10, 2020. verywellmind.com/delayed-onset-ptsd-meaning-and-reasons-2797636

Worrall, Simon. "Venomous Animals Kill in Horrible Ways—and Also Cure." *National Geographic.* September 18, 2016. nationalgeographic.com/news/2016/09/venomous-deadliest-creatures-cure-christie-wilcox

Rosenberg, Ross. *The Human Magnet Syndrome: Why We Love People Who Hurt Us.* Dublin, Ireland: Premier Publisher & Media, 2013.

Bendiksen, Ashley. Interview by author, November 2019.

Christensen, Karen. Interview by author, November 2019.

## CHALLENGE 8: SMALLS & CHOOSE YOUR BATTLEGROUND

Lineberry, Cate. *Be Free or Die: The Amazing Story of Robert Smalls' Escape from Slavery to Union Hero.* New York: St. Martin's Press, 2017.

Gates, Henry Louis. "Which Slave Sailed Himself to Freedom?" PBS, The African Americans: Many Rivers to Cross. Accessed January 3, 2019. pbs.org/wnet/african-americans-many-rivers-to-cross/history/which-slave-sailed-himself-to-freedom

Reilly, Lucas. "Robert Smalls: The Slave Who Stole a Confederate Warship and Became a Congressman." *MentalFloss.* February 12, 2019. mentalfloss.com/article/91630/robert-smalls-slave-who-stole-confederate-warship-and-became-congressman

Anthony, Dave, and Reynolds, Gareth. "Robert Smalls." The Dollop #326. Audio podcast. podcasts.apple.com/us/podcast/326-robert-smalls/id643055307?i=1000410929052

Moore, Michael B. "The Audacity of Robert Smalls." TEDx St.MarksSchool. November 6, 2015. youtube.com/watch?v=w6T7ksyhUkw

Lineberry, Cate. "The Thrilling Tale of How Robert Smalls Seized a Confederate Ship and Sailed it to Freedom." *Smithsonian Magazine.* June 13, 2017. smithsonianmag.com/history/thrilling-tale-how-robert-smalls-heroically-sailed-stolen-confederate-ship-freedom-180963689

"Sex and Gender Differences in Substance Use." National Institutes of Health—National Institute on Drug Abuse. Last updated July 2018. drugabuse.gov/publications/research-reports/substance-use-in-women/sex-gender-differences-in-substance-use

"Violence in the Media and Entertainment." Position Paper of the American Academy of Family Physicians. Last updated 2016. aafp.org/about/policies/all/violence-media.html

# DEFINING YOUR RITE OF PASSAGE

Michler, Ryan. "Creating a Rite of Passage, Becoming More Decisive, and Your One Objective as a Leader." Order of Man: Reclaiming and Restoring Masculinity—Ask Me Anything. Audio podcast. podcasts.apple.com/us/podcast/creating-rite-passage-becoming-more-decisive-your-one/id979752171?i=1000419589495

Le Corre, Erwan. "Finding Purpose and Rites of Passage." Daniel Vitalis Presents ReWild Yourself #56." Audio podcast. podcasts.apple.com/us/podcast/finding-purpose-and-rites-of-passage-erwan-le-corre-56/id892905009?i=1000347702513

Michler, Ryan. "Building a Rite of Passage." *Order of Man: Reclaiming and Restoring Masculinity.* June 30, 2017. orderofman.com/building-rite-of-passage

# ACKNOWLEDGMENTS

## WHO'S MY BATTLE CREW?

This is the Battle Crew of behind-the-scenes True Warriors who fought alongside me to make this book a reality . . . in the order they entered the book's creation story.

**Sara Sargent,** my editor at Penguin Random House: If there's anyone in the world I'd ask to be stuck in an egg with, it'd be you. ¯\\_(ツ)_/¯ You were the genesis of this book, and it's your Warrior heart that allowed you to summon it from the ether and make it a thing that exists. Look, if Thor's hammer was real, that would definitely be your Warrior weapon due to the quality of your heart. Your job is to tell kids the best stories and craft those stories to be the best they can be. *That* is a thing of beauty. Even cooler? You're the best in the world at it. I came to you metaphorically fumbling a pile of four hundred loose pages that were totally out of order and falling on the floor. The pages that weren't missing were filled with sentences that made no sense. Somehow you saw through it and—literally and figuratively—reorganized and carved out a book with voice and clarity and readability (IMHO). You took a pretty huge risk on me . . . and had you not brought a lifetime of education, career, and human experience, it would be greatly lacking from what it has now become. Not to mention, without you, it wouldn't exist. You made it happen. It's your message as much as mine. It was a great joy to essentially enter an art studio with a random stranger, then sit down with her and paint on the same canvas. Only catch? We weren't allowed to talk about anything except what's most important to our hearts. Then, when the artwork was finished, we went back to our routines. That's what we did here. You are a mighty True Warrior, by every definition and trait we landed on.

**Josh Shipp,** my manager at Top Youth Speakers: I'm pretty sure your personal Warrior Creed is "I'm gonna figure out how to make my wildest, craziest dreams become reality. Then I'm gonna help other people do that for themselves, too." And Josh? You do. It's humbling and inspiring and jaw-dropping to see your battle tactics at work. To everyone, it looks like you pull opportunities out of thin air. Hate to spoil your magic trick . . . but I know that it took a lifetime of "doing the work," plus a lot of platform-building bricklaying, before you became the guy who can make that happen. Thank you for your life's work, for inviting me to the TYS family, and for believing in me—through friendship, by our professional relationship, and as a brother of common spirit. You brought this book opportunity to me and believed I was the right guy for the job. Then you supported me all the way through. I'm deeply grateful for you.

**Erin Niumata,** my agent from Folio Literary Management: The snowstorm was so strong, my hotel room window was shaking. The phone rang and you made me laugh like crazy, in a way that I wasn't sure if I was allowed to be laughing or not, because it was a professional conversation, which made me laugh even harder. I heard your love for your son in that conversation, and somehow I could just *feel* that this project was important to you. I hung up the phone, thinking, "This woman gets things done." And you did. You made this a reality and somehow figured out how to put my name on a contract with a dream publisher. You crushed it.

**Dave Tieche:** You were among the first to read my wild setup, and you had the imagination, passion, and technical skill to whip it into shape. Your feedback and encouragement made me believe that I might actually have the writing prowess to pull this thing off well. You're the man, dude.

**Tyson Hale:** We were on a climbing road trip when the ball started rolling for this book. We drove hours away from climbing crags to reach cell service, just so I could get some calls out to New York. In our Zion/Arches/Grand Staircase/Moab/Vegas loop, we talked about manhood, cultural understandings of masculinity and femininity, and how to live an honorable life, all while doing manly stuff, being goons, and revisiting what it was like to be boys. You're a great friend, and your lifelong influence on me has made a big influence on the content in this book.

**Sasha Henriques:** You helped me figure out how to say what I wanted to say. That is a true gift that you give people. Not only that, but how to say it so that kids (and adults!) might read those thoughts. Your hard-earned insight into our culture and world and into experiences I'm not privy to helped point out many of my blind spots. Thank you for courageously, and correctly, communicating the ways my thought process and writing could be honed. I have a hunch that you've gone to bat for me and this project more times than I realize, and I'm immensely grateful for that. Your encouragement, insights, heart, passion, and concerns, and even the giant flags you posted, all accurately pointed the way. You made me a better human through this work we did.

**Johnny Dombrowski:** You absolutely crushed it with the cover and interior art. During the writing process, when I came to those blank pages each day, man, I'd see your creations and be inspired. In fact, I started dozens of writing days by opening your design files, and they gave me life. Your work makes the eight-year-old kid in me feel stupidly excited to crawl under the covers and read with a flashlight. It sends the thirteen-year-old kid in me on an adventurous escape. Overall, your art captures the beauty and the passion I'm trying to tell kids is in the world. And it brings a deeper meaning of purpose, values, and grit to the book. Your illustrations and cover design are perfect. You really, really killed it. Thank you for all the dedication, revisions, skill, and passion that went into them.

**Steve Hemmann:** You cruised around Oregon with me for ten days in a camper van as we talked about what it means to be a man. We were method acting, doing the manliest stuff either of us could think of. You helped me to get in the writing zone—and helped me to stay there—for many months, by getting me to actually sit down and write out the stuff that made the most sense. You and that trip helped to create the skeleton of this beast. A lot of its DNA came from the savage beast of a man who you are. Many of your thoughts and concepts went right into this bad boy, and that's because you live and think as a fine example of a great man. You're a flippin' rad Battle Crew member, dude, and a Warrior in every sense of the word.

Warrior professionals whose time, knowledge, expertise, and wisdom had a direct impact on the book's content: **Dr. Mithu Storoni,** MA (Cantab), MB BChir, MRCOphth, PhD; **Ashley Bendiksen; Jessie Funk,** LCSW; **Shannon Thomas,** LCSW-S; **Karen Christensen,** LPC, LSOTP; **Dr. Jeff Wood,** PhD; **Dr. Scott Rower,** PhD; **Kimberly Martin,** LPC; and **Morgan Mitchell,** Registered Trauma Counselor (BPsych) EMDR. Your time, guidance, counseling, wisdom, training, and studies influenced this project in significant ways.

And of course, the dozens of wonderful people in my tribes who discussed content ideas with me and put up with my writing schedule: the **Kite sisters, Katie Goodwin, Lauren Allison, Hijos Del Tinto, Kaspar Paur, TYS Family, Chris Abbey, Jim Ponder and our Kili Team, Team Germany,** and the **LeVerdiers**!

Pre-readers and opinion givers on the rough draft, **Ed Seaman, Brian Williams, Janae Rowberry, Jennifer Earl-Norton, Jennifer Spooner-Hunt, Laura Christensen, Kevin Tucker, Jessica Pope, David Flood, Chris Abbey, Joshua Wayne, Kyle Scheeley, Shane Feldman, Bridget Kruger, Adam Stramwasser, Dr. Laymon Hicks, Blake Fly, EJ Carrion, Fabian Ramirez, Naomi Snyder,** and **Sara Shipp.**

Of course, there are the featured Warrior friends of mine whose lives you've experienced just small pieces of: **Viorel "Wally" Stirbu, Kakuta Hamisi, Dennis Hollenbeck,** and **Sandra Nett.** Your lives, your feats, your wisdom, and your decisions have greatly impacted who I am as a person, and I hope in turn many young men.

Historical Warriors whom I'd be honored to meet: **Danny Way, Kevin Jorgeson, Terry Crews,** and were it possible, **Ernest Shackleton** and **Robert Smalls.** You blow me away. What you've done, the legacies you've created, and the approaches you've taken to your respective challenges inspire me to be, act, and think as a better man. I did my darnedest to use your actual quotes and represent your thoughts and beliefs, per the media and sources I scoured the earth to find on each of you.

I'd also be very remiss to not say this . . . I've learned immensely from the people who have experienced me when I haven't lived up to the ideals presented here. This stuff I talk about here took time to figure out. I messed up along the way. I still do. A lot. If you're one of the people I've somehow hurt during my journey and we don't speak anymore, I'd like to make clear: This book is me publicly saying, "Here's what I learned from the mistakes I recognize I've made and how I've tried my best to be a better person for others." If by any chance you're reading this, I'm sorry again, and I hope your life is beautiful.

That also goes for EVERYONE who's been a part of my life who wasn't a part of the creation of this puppy. I know I can be a bumpy Warrior to be around sometimes. I'm trying. And I love you guys.

**My Team at Random House:** This has been such a dream, and I am so grateful to everyone who made it happen. For making the cover and interior amazing, April Ward. For copyediting and keeping this book on schedule, Alison Kolani. For being patient with my process and giving us the gift of time, Janet Foley. For your wise comments, Renée Cafiero. For your thoughtful read and feedback, Lois Evans. For supporting Sara's and my vision, Michelle Nagler and Mallory Loehr. For seeing through all the promo and marketing of the book, the Publicity, Marketing, and School & Library Marketing teams.

Finally, there's my Family Battle Crew . . .

**Mom and Dad:** The endless support you give is as awe-inspiring as your forty-nine years of marriage. You both tell me, "You'll always be our son, no matter what." My reply? "I'll always admire you two to no end, no matter what."

**Mike and Jackie:** You two are a rock for me, my brother and SILY! As I was writing this, I also painted a van in the driveway of your brand-new home and totally crashed your pad for a bit of your first year of marriage. If that's not support, I don't know what is.

**The Johnstons:** My love is with all of you, always. You inspired me to bring a fire of passion to this project.

**Jenny:** So fun hanging with your Battle Crew in The Bob while working on this! Love you!

**Sadie:** Thanks for taking me on walks, pawing at me when I needed a break from writing, and being there for cuddles when I was facing the tough stuff this book required. You smelly, furry beast—I couldn't ask for a better dog.

Without the humans I've met in my life, I would not exist as I am today. In some way or another, we all made this book together. Thank you, Warriors, for making art with me. I love you all.

**JOHN BEEDE** is a mountaineer, global adventurer, humanitarian, and keynote speaker. He has climbed the tallest mountain on all seven continents, including Mount Everest. He's also been struck by lightning, been attacked by a five-foot iguana, and gone swimming with great white sharks. His travels have taken him to more than seventy countries and he's survived every classification of natural disaster. Through it all, John's core message to the kids he speaks to and teaches is that we live by the strength of our morals and values, not our accomplishments. He has shared this message via motivational presentations and workshops to nearly one million live audience members in all fifty U.S. states and all across the world. He has given keynote speeches for national teen organizations including 4-H, FCCLA, FBLA, DECA, BPA, SkillsUSA, ScoutsUSA, FFA, Teen Institute, and the National Association of Student Councils. John is also the author of *Climb On! Success Strategies for Teens* and *The Mini-Manual for Becoming Super Awesome*. He is an Eagle Scout and he graduated with a bachelor's degree in mass communications from Wheaton College. John lives in Nevada. Find him on Twitter at @johnbeede, on Instagram at @johnbeede, and online at johnbeede.com.